I Want My Son Back

5/2-2/ 2003

Routaya,

Best wishes

Rob Carey

I Want My Son Back

❖

The Harrowing True Story of a Father's Fight for Custody

Robert Carey
with Rusty Fischer

iUniverse, Inc.
New York Lincoln Shanghai

I Want My Son Back
The Harrowing True Story of a Father's Fight for Custody

iUniverse, Inc.

For information address:
iUniverse, Inc.
2021 Pine Lake Road, Suite 100
Lincoln, NE 68512
www.iuniverse.com

Note: Names with an asterisk (*) have been changed to protect the innocent…

ISBN: 0-595-27390-4

Printed in the United States of America

I wish to dedicate this book to the memory of Linda Severina Carey. She lived her life beautifully as a child of God and a believer in the Lord Jesus Christ. In the few years we shared together, we ran the full gamut of loving, living, serving one another, and then dying. She showed me faith. She showed me love. She showed me the most beautiful traits that any woman could ever reveal. Most of all she poured her life into mine—and our son's. All that Michael and I are inside is because of what God did through the life of Linda Severina Carey. I am blessed to have known her. Michael and I will always carry a part of her in our hearts...

Contents

Acknowledgements

I want to acknowledge the assistance and support of all my friends, family, and church family. Without their love, encouragement, and emotional support, I would not have been able to survive this "trail of trials." My father has been a source of encouragement all the days of my life. When I have had to face the most difficult ordeals, I knew that I could call upon him and he would be there for me.

I also want to recognize Linda's father, Gus Nelson, who has been a source of strength more often than he realizes. He knew how much I loved his daughter, Linda. He knew how hard I worked to care for her and Michael as she lay on her deathbed. He would call to check in with me and tell me that he loved me. Next to my own father, I have so much gratitude for Gus Nelson's support in the days following Linda's death—and even more so now. It has come with a price, because in the divorce his own granddaughter, Kimberly Dunn (Linda's daughter), turned on me and became a part of the continuing plot to steal Michael away from me.

I especially want to acknowledge my wife, Lisa, who has been my faithful friend and source of great encouragement. No one on this earth knows me more completely and loves me more thoroughly than she does. She has helped me by being a sounding board in my frustration. She has helped me edit my communications. All of her efforts have come with a price, too, because she has had to endure a considerable amount of hardship in the process of our relationship. I am blessed to know, and be well known, by two great women in my lifetime, Linda and now Lisa.

Foreword:
Blind Justice by Lisa Carey

I remember when my husband, Robert, told me that Michael wasn't coming home. That his ex-wife, deemed the "psychological parent" by the Benton county court system, had been given sole and legal custody of his son. Of *his* son! I was incredulous that this had happened to Rob, to us, to *Michael*.

An uneasy feeling gripped my whole body as I convulsed, finally giving into my tears. It had been such a long battle, against an enemy that shouldn't have even been given credibility by the courts in the first place.

How could the judicial system in this country, one that went out of its way to speak out in favor of so-called "family values," give a person custody of a child that was never hers to begin with? How could they take a child from his very own father? The father that loved him more than life itself, and never once neglected or abused him?

I once thought I had all the answers.

But now all I have are *questions*…

We are a "blended family" that once counted five…but now we are only four. Our story will amaze and astound you as you weave through the trials and tribulations of a biological father seeking the rightful custody of his son. A son that he was given full legal and physical custody of following a long and bitter divorce. A son that was lost to him, and finally given over to a former *step*mother, based on lies and the expert manipulation of a legal system gone awry.

I can't begin to express the pain, the sorrow, the betrayal, the disillusionment, the *anger* that follows after having any contact with the woman in question. I give my husband comfort as best I can, but what he *really* wants is to hold his son, Michael, again. He wants to watch his son grow into a young man, capable of making it on his own in this complicated world. He wants to be a daily part of his son's life, and wants his son to experience what love is like in a Christian family.

Every now and then I ask myself "what if" questions, but nothing changes…

Daily, we muster the strength to go on—because this journey is far from over. Though the legal options have been diminished, the hostilities between both sides continue unabated. Rob's ex-wife does not appear to be content until she has completely destroyed every tie Michael has with his biological family, and grafted him into her family, as if he was an orphan.

In the midst of daily discouragement, we make our personal struggle public in order to sound the alarm. There is a growing movement of law in certain states that can—and regularly *does*—take away parents' custodial rights.

We want this book to stand as a testament of truth—for Michael. Michael has a right to know and to understand how hard we fought for his return to our family. *His* family. We believe, in the end, that it is the truth that will eventually set this young captive free.

I realize there is a risk involved in the publication of this book. I believe Rob's ex-wife will retaliate by further manipulation of people in legal authority who will not like having their "dirty laundry" exposed.

In fact, the very real possibility exists that those in authority may even attempt to take away *all* contact that we currently have with Michael. We cannot let these fears overpower us.

We must give our fears over to God, and rise above them…

We believe there are other people, other families out there, who are at risk of being torn apart as we have been, and we must get the word out in any way we can.

This is our attempt to do just that…

Introduction:
How Did We Get Here?

No one ever falls in love, thinking they're going to fall *out* of love. No one ever says, "I love you" with their fingers crossed. No one ever proposes with a fake diamond ring, or signs their love notes with and "x," but no "o"!

In short, no one ever *thinks* they'll become a divorce statistic. Everyone always thinks they'll be the one to beat the odds and see it through to their 50th wedding anniversary, when they'll throw a huge party in a lavish ballroom, surrounded by family, friends—and a room full of envious divorcees.

Even those angry, embattled couples you always see fighting in restaurants, shouting in malls, stalking off from one another in hotel lobbies—even those couples you *know* are doomed for divorce—at one time or another they both cared so deeply about each other that they couldn't stand to live apart.

No one ever gets married…thinking they're going to get *divorced.*

And no one with children *ever* gets married lightly. It is a double bond, a sacred selection, for not only are you marrying someone for yourself—but for your child, or your children, as well. Careful consideration is taken to ensure that not only are you choosing a perfect mate, but a perfect *parent* in the bargain. And, let's face it, nobody's "perfect" these days. In today's world, love comes in all shapes and sizes, incomes and ages, temperaments and personalities.

Some people would go so far as to say *every* marriage is a risk.

Others would say that *every* divorce is inevitable…

The truth is, in this country, dozens of marriages occur *every* day. Every *day!* Unfortunately, nearly just as many get divorced: 48% of all married couples, to be exact. Like those stats? How about these:

- Percentage of weddings which are remarriages for at least one partner: **43%**

- Percentage of first marriages that end in divorce: **50%**

- Percentage of remarriages that end in divorce: **60%**

- Percentage of divorced women who remarry within five years: **54%**

- Estimated average length of divorce proceedings: **1 year!**

As reported by the **US Census Bureau** in the late 90s, children of divorce were 50% more likely than their counterparts from in tact families to eventually divorce themselves. In nineteen states reporting such custody matters in the late 90s: 72% of child custody cases were awarded to the wife, while only 9% were awarded to the husband. In 16% of such cases, joint custody was awarded.

Meanwhile, fatherless homes account for 63% of youth suicides in this country, 90% of all homeless children or runaways, 85% of children with both minor and severe behavior problems, 71% of high school dropouts, 85% of youths in prison, and well over 50% of today's teen mothers.

It is painfully clear that divorce is just one more of those "sad but true" facts of modern day American life, both for the adults involved and, unfortunately, for the children as well. What should also be painfully clear by this point is that quite a few divorces get downright nasty. Throw child custody hearings into the mix, and they get even nastier!

No one ever gets married…thinking they're going to get divorced. And no father enters into a marriage, let alone a *second* marriage, thinking that he's going to eventually have to fork over his own son to his ex-wife.

I never, ever wanted to get a divorce. But it happened to me. And it can happen to you, too. I am a father—without a son. Michael is my son—without a father. We don't live together anymore.

Here's why…

Prologue:
Looking Forward, Looking Back

There is a secret I keep from my beautiful new wife, Lisa. Not the bad kind, the kind that could eventually break up a loving marriage such as ours. But not really the good kind, either. It's the kind of secret a devoted husband keeps from his wife because he doesn't want to worry her, because she's already worried enough, because he wants to keep her from that which is unpleasant, scary, sad, and tragic. Because he wants to protect her. Shield her.

Perhaps, just maybe, it's more of an addiction, really, than a secret at all. Not an obsession, technically. But a physical addiction, a craving that washes over me from time to time—albeit quite regularly these days—and forces me to leave our wedding bed before the sun rises over our cozy little neighborhood in Plano, Texas.

I rise steadily, slowly, so our queen-sized bed won't creak or moan. I stand there, just at the foot of the warm, cozy bed, letting my eyes adjust to the pre-dawn darkness, listening to Lisa's breathing, watching the sheets over her chest rise and fall, fall and rise, with the steadiness of her blissful, uninterrupted sleep.

When I'm absolutely sure that she's not startled by my movements, when I'm sure I haven't awakened her too early for work, when I'm sure she's still soundly asleep, I step quietly into my trusty slippers and inch into my threadbare robe before secreting myself out of our bedroom and into the hall.

Carefully, ever so carefully, wending my way around the various furnishings inside this old, Texas house, I pass silently the rooms of my precious stepchildren, Shannon and Derrick, careful to pause just past each doorway—listening intently for signs of life, for the creaking of a bed or the rustling of sheets or the shuffling of bare, pink feet on carpet.

Only when I'm sure the house is fast asleep, only when I'm confident that no one will arise from slumber to catch me in my tiny, little secret, do I look in upon the bedroom that Michael used to share with his stepbrother, Derrick. Two twin beds separated by a walk in closet door dominate the small room. Michael's things are just as he left them. His shelves holding his books, his stuffed animals, his videos. On his bed is his Digimon comforter and pillow, with a stuffed toy Santa Claus nestled just so.

On the walls are pictures of little Michael with his mother Linda and I before she got so sick—and passed away. There are mementos of Michael's on the wall—drawings, ribbons, posters—and a framed display of all the awards I received as a Cub Scout, Boy Scout, and when I was in the US Navy—badges from bobcat to eagle, 26 merit badges, ribbons, and medals in all.

All these things had been a part of what Michael had surrounded himself with. A part of his mornings, his afternoon, his evenings. Until that fateful day when a vengeful voice from his past manipulated the law and had Child Protective Services take him into custody—even as she had his own father jailed on false charges.

Everything remained on Michael's side of that bedroom, just as it had been the day he left. Everything he had known, everything that gave him comfort, everything that was so *familiar* to little Michael was right there waiting for him.

But where was Michael?

And, more importantly, would he ever be allowed to return?

There is an emptiness in this little boy's room, the same emptiness that fills his father's heart. This is my son's room. Michael's room. This is not a bad dream; this is real—and it hurts *every* day.

The bed itself has a history: It belonged to Michael's great grandmother, Severina Nelson. She slept in it until her death. Michael's own mother had it in her home for many years. It has been Michael's bed since he graduated from his crib, just about the time his own mother died.

Next to his bed is a bureau with three drawers. Inside the bureau, were anyone to take a peek, they would find seven pairs of small underwear, seven pairs of plain white tube socks, and a small assortment of shorts and sweat pants—each pair as brand new as the next. All as stiff and bright and colorful and clean as the day on which they were purchased. Inside a closet that dominates the back center of the room, were someone to look inside, they would find a few unworn T-shirts, a coat, sweaters, and shirts of various colors, sizes, and styles hanging on pristine hangers.

Just in case…

On the top of the bureau, a stuffed lion with his cub—"Michael and dad," as he used to put it—sits next to a single color picture in a simple, wooden frame. Though the picture is large, a full 8 x 10, it wasn't expensive: Just a few extra dollars from my wallet during school picture time a year or two back. But well worth it to a father.

A father with a secret…

I enter the room now, very quietly. Tiptoeing in, barely breathing, closing the door behind me without a single noise. No click of the lock, no turning of the handle. The only sounds are my breathing, my heart pounding, my slippered feet sliding on carpet, and perhaps the whispering of my robe against the side of the comforter as I finally allow myself to crumble onto a corner of the bed and hang my head in my hands.

My thoughts are always the same: I think of the past.

A past filled with love and fondness, hope and dreams…

I was a simple husband and loving father, once upon a time in a world that now seems so very far away. Living a simple life with my wife and young son. Next to my smiling picture in some fantasy dictionary, I always secretly believed, there would be printed the caption, "The Happy Family," followed by a dictionary definition filled with words like "laughter," "desire," "trust," and "faith."

Life was as it should be, in every way, on every day: A man and a woman fall in love, court properly, get married, and have a beautiful child, a precious son. It doesn't matter, not a whit, that this son, Michael, is autistic. Doesn't matter that a loving wife and devoted mother, a wife and mother named Linda, comes down with cancer shortly thereafter.

After all, what is life if not struggle?

What is struggle…if not *life*?

Challenges came and went along the path of our tiny trio, but we always faced them together, as a family, as partners in some grand scheme, as a team committed to the needs and desires of one another. I knew my son would overcome his challenging disability one day. I knew my wife would eventually beat her cancer. I had no doubt in my mind that our lives would one day return to normal and that things would be as they were. That things would be as they *should* be.

And for a little while longer, at least, things held together—just as they should. Just as we had planned.

But slowly, inevitably, the seams of our happy life began unraveling like the hem of a favorite sweater. The hours-long surgery Linda endured to eradicate her cancer was horrendous, but we fought on. The radiation and chemotherapy treatments Linda received to wipe out her cancer cells made her feel worse, not better. Still, we fought on. In short order the treatments to stem the tide of this wretched disease caused more hospitalizations and yet, we fought on. We refused to let go of our hope.

We refused to lose sight of our dream.

We fought on and we fought side by side—until there was little left to do but accept the inevitable…

We are never really ready for the end. I know this now. We don't want to let go of the life we hold so dear, but there is a time when love commands that we must do the very thing we hate. In this case, I had to tell the woman I loved more than my own life a lie. I had to tell her that Michael and I would be okay. I had to let her know it was okay to let go, to be free—and go on to heaven.

I knew it would hurt more than I could bear, but I could *not* think of myself at such a crucial time. My love for Linda commanded that I release her from the emotional and physical torment brought on by cancer, even if it meant our parting words were filled with lies. Sweet, perhaps bittersweet, little white lies…

Life without Linda was almost unbearable, almost not worth living, *almost*…but only because of the living legacy she had left behind: My precious son, Michael. Michael became my refuge, my home, my one and only love. Pastors, family, friends, they were all a satisfying comfort to me—but Michael was my heart. My soul. My light…

And thus began a slow, rocky time of health and healing for us both. Father *and* son. A time of recovery, of wonder, of falling in love all over again…with each other. I got to know my son the way few men ever get to know any of their children. Despite his autism—Michael is extremely high-functioning—we never failed to be able to communicate with one another on a deeper level. He knew my heart, I knew his.

Together, we made an unbeatable team…

But between the bedtime stories and picnic lunches, between the videos and double-features, between the cookies and long, Sunday breakfasts of pancakes and applesauce, I began to feel that something was missing from Michael's young, impressionable life. Despite what popular TV sitcoms and *Cosmopolitan* magazine may have to say on the subject, a child needs more than one parent—this I knew.

The sadness in Michael's little eyes when he went to look at the bed his parents once shared, the wandering look he gave other mothers at church, in the grocery store, at the mall—was more than just missing Linda. A boy needs a mother. And, in those few quiet moments I did manage to wrangle for myself at the end of another long, emotional day, another thought occurred to me as well: A man needs a wife.

And so, eager to make our house a loving home once again, I entered the single world of blind dates and "meet and greets" a new man, with a new title: widower. Seeking the counsel of my pastor and his wife, I began writing to a woman who came with the utmost recommendation from her own pastor and his wife as a potential wife for me—and a mother for young Michael.

A beautiful and charming woman, middle-aged like myself, who would eventually wrap me under her tantalizing spell.

A woman who would first capture my heart, and then my hand—in marriage.

A woman who would take Michael into her own life as surely as she did myself.

A woman who would turn out to be something quite different from the tender and caring lady I opened my heart—and my son's life—to.

A woman who would soon make my life, and Michael's, miserable.

A woman to whom, eventually, marriage was no longer possible, and divorce the only option.

A woman so blinded by the deadly sins of greed and pride that she would lie to the Benton County District Attorney's office, the local police, and even the grand jury in her quest for custody, separation of father from child, and child support.

A woman who would hire a costly private investigator, if only to see me thrown in jail like some common criminal.

A woman who would succeed in not only having me arrested, but taking from me the one thing that truly mattered in my life—my only son.

By the time I look up and dry my eyes on the sleeve of my old, familiar robe, the sun is slowly rising outside Derrick and Michael's single window and the first, faint strains of a waking family are due to erupt in the loving house around me at any moment. It's not fair to share my secret with them. It's not fair to let the battles of my past invade the peace of this warm, quiet house.

And so I smooth the rumpled corner of the comforter, straighten the framed picture of young Michael on the top of the dresser, and exit the room just as quietly as I had entered only a few, fragile minutes before.

Another day is ready to start.

Another day, full of life, hope, promise, relief, sadness, guilt, regret, and always, *always* constant sorrow.

Another day under the hot Texas sun.

Another day to grow and learn as a man, as a husband, as a…father.

Another day…without my son.

1

Love, Interrupted

o o o o o o o o o o o o o o o o o o o o o o o o o o o o o o o o o o o

Two are better than one…If one person falls, the other can reach out and help. But people who are alone when they fall are in real trouble. And on a cold night, two under the same blanket can gain warmth from each other. But how can one be warm alone? A person standing alone can be attacked and defeated, but two can stand back-to-back and conquer. Three are even better, for a triple-braided cord is not easily broken.

—Ecclesiastes 4:9-12

It was the spring of 1989. I had just finished my third college degree the year before and was working full-time as an auditor for the state of Washington. Most of my life was as it should be. The pieces were falling into place. Yet, in those few, rare, quiet moments I allowed myself between my US Naval Reserve classes, my state auditing travels, and my church activities, I knew that I could no longer lie to myself any longer: There *was* something missing.

I knew exactly what it was, of course: I wanted a woman to share my life with. A friend to go share my travels with, a woman to share my faith-filled convictions with, a companion at my side on countless dinner dates, lazy Sunday afternoons, and the coming holiday season. A partner in my hopes and dreams, an investor in my heart, a shareholder in my future—*our* future.

I wanted a lover, a friend, a buddy, a pal, a roommate, a companion—a *wife*.

With a schedule as hectic and busy as mine, however, I knew no one would come tripping over me on a quick lunch break or a long drive home, and so I started actively doing some things to bring me in contact with women as mature and spiritual as myself. Slowly, I began taking advantage of the personal columns and began writing several honest, realistic ads in search of love and commitment. As a result, I soon began to go on several dates.

Many of the women I met during this exciting, yet awkward, time were pretty, or smart, or funny, or caring, or sexy, or independent, or compassionate—but rarely all, or even several, of those attractive qualities at the very same time. Some were much too eager, others were way too shy. Some were too flashy and bold, others were wiry wallflowers. Few held enough interest for me to request a second date, and, I'm quite sure, the feeling was occasionally mutual. It wasn't fun to be on the dating trail, but I knew it was a necessary evil were I to find commitment and compassion for my golden years.

Still, several of the women I dated stood out from the bustling crowd and I slowly began pursuing one or two in earnest. Likewise, one or two even pursued me back! One of the ladies I had dated casually a few times eventually began pressing me for a bigger commitment, but I knew in my heart that she was not the one I was looking for. And so, eventually, after chasing down false leads again and again and invariably finding myself at some lonely dead end, I would once again return to ground zero and start the whole process all over again.

In September of 1989 I ran across an advertisement in a singles newspaper about a Christian organization where single people could meet by blind mailbox and, eventually, even set up a meeting in person if they so desired. The organization was called the Church of Many Mansions, or CMM, for short. It operated on the generous donations of its members and the mutual respect of mature adults of both sexes.

Shrugging my shoulders and expecting yet another round of disappointment and heartache, I submitted my carefully written personal ad and, in response, got a listing of several hundred ads similarly written by women looking for men.

Finally, I ran across one that caught my eye…

Her ad read: "Widow, 40, Caucasian, blonde hair, blue eyes, 5'9," height/weight proportionate, very athletic, no children at home, desire same; retired; Assembly of God church; Issaquah, WA."

We were the same age. The fact that she was active in the Assembly of God church further interested me, because I was a member of an Assembly of God church in Tacoma, Washington. Our physical statistics were even similar: I am 6'6", slender, with blonde hair and blue eyes.

She lived in a city about 90 miles from me, but the distance was not a deterrent. She sounded like someone I would like to get to know more about. I eagerly sat down and wrote a letter to her via the Church of Many Mansions blind mailbox.

In due time she not only received it, but responded in kind by saying that she would like to meet with me. In her response she included her phone number, the best time of day to call, and finally gave me her name: Linda.

Linda. Feeling the first, eager twinge of anticipation, I quickly suggested a neutral location in Issaquah so that she could feel more comfortable at our first meeting. (Both of us were cautious about calling it a "date!") Also, I had learned from experience that this was a good "out" for us both, just in case: If either of us saw that the meeting was not working out, then we could easily go our separate ways without the awkwardness of a long car drive back to her place or mine.

Fortunately, such precautions hadn't been necessary…

Linda and I met at a warm, cozy pizza place and both of us immediately liked what we saw. After a short time it was getting too noisy in the crowded restaurant for us to visit as we wished, so I asked her if we could go somewhere else a little more peaceful. Since it was so close and our meeting had gone so well, Linda suggested that we should just go up to her place.

In her beautiful home overlooking Lake Sammamish, we had hot tea and warm conversation for several pleasant hours. When it was finally time for me to leave, I asked to see her again and Linda said she would like that as well. I told her I was going on a trip to see family in Massachusetts, but that I would like to take her out when I got back later the next week. She readily agreed and I eagerly marked down the date on my formerly empty social calendar.

When I had returned from my travels, we went out for dinner in the middle of the week, neither of us wanting to wait until the coming weekend. I really enjoyed being with Linda and she seemed to enjoy herself with me. Before the evening was over I asked to see her again the following weekend. She said that she had some previous plans, but that she could see me for a few hours during the day on Saturday. When I arrived, it turned out that she had surprised me by canceling her previous engagement!

That meant that we had the whole day and evening to ourselves…

As the following weeks passed by in a flurry of couples activity, I soon realized that I really, really liked Linda. I knew that I was developing much stronger feelings for her as well. Stronger than friendship. Stronger than mere companionship. Stronger feelings, in fact, than I had felt in a good, long while.

I knew what they were leading up to. I think that she did, too.

One day we went to the museum, and later that afternoon she roller-skated while I rode my bike around the lake in the park. We went out for dinner later that same night. Before I left her that evening, I took a big step and asked her if I could kiss her.

She said, "yes."

That kiss was like no other kiss I had ever had in my life. It was indescribably sweet and tenderly inviting. That one kiss told me that she cared for me as well. It both thrilled me and frightened me with the heady mix of emotions it stirred within me. All that next week, while on US Naval Reserve active duty, I couldn't get her off my mind.

It was like the crushes I had felt in high school all over again!

I struggled and prayed about what I was feeling, wondering if I should share with her my feelings or not. It was an ongoing struggle in my mind for days on end. Finally, I felt compelled to simply tell her. I called her as soon as I could and told her that I was falling in love with her. Unfortunately, her response was not what I had hoped for: she didn't say anything one way or the other. I thought I had probably blown it by being too bold, too forthright, too soon.

"Way to go, Rob," I thought miserably that night.

The next weekend Linda had asked me to escort her to a dinner that some friends had planned for her at the Space Needle Restaurant in Seattle. By the time I got to her house on the appointed day, I was very unsure of myself and just as unsure about what Linda was feeling. Like an impetuous teenager I felt that I had rushed too far, too soon, and couldn't help but feel embarrassed as I pulled up to her house.

When I finally arrived she gave me a warm hug and a gentle kiss at the front door and my nervousness slowly began to dissipate. We went for a drive around the nearby lake to calm our frazzled nerves. While I drove I nervously talked about myself, my words tumbling over themselves as they seemed to take on a life of their own. In the rush of frenzied sentences and phrases I related some errors I had made during my life and said, "I guess I have had to learn from my mistakes."

In reply, she said something that seemed very profound to me at the time: "The only thing we learn from our mistakes is how to do things *wrong*."

I immediately pulled the car over and told her how impressed I was with her frankness, maturity, and honesty. In that moment, perhaps implying some kind of lasting relationship, I asked her to *always* be direct with me. I then told her that I loved her. She turned to me, her kind and gentle face smiling bashfully, and said that she loved me, too. Instinctually I kissed her and held her close. I was nervous, but in a different way than I had been before we talked. Now my nervousness was not caused by fear of failure, but instead it was replaced with a new reason for butterflies: excitement!

It was hard to play low-key that evening around her friends and later on, when they had finally left, it was so nice to have her all to myself again. It was difficult to leave at the end of that evening and have to wait for four whole days before I would see her again. I guess that's the moment I knew I was hooked!

We continued to write and call each other every couple of days. Just like a little child bemused by the inconsistent physics of Christmas, the time between seeing her seemed to go so *slow* and yet, while we were together, the time went so terribly *fast*.

There's a love song by sultry soul singer Sade that goes, "every day is Christmas, and every night—is New Year's Eve…" I guess that's a little like what it felt to date Linda: The holiday highs when we were together, the holiday *blues* when we were apart!

As our relationship grew, we set mutually agreeable ground rules in our budding courtship. In essence, unlike so many other modern dating couples, we would keep ourselves pure before the Lord. There would be no form of touching in any sexual way. I would come down to spend the weekend each week, but I would spend Friday and Saturday nights at a local motel each and every time.

Without the unnecessary frustration of sexual matters, we were left with precious time to be focused on our mutual needs, our likes, our dislikes. It gave us time to get to know each other, instead of simply "getting into bed." Eventually, we began to talk about the future. Initially, there was some concern from our various family members about how quickly our relationship seemed to be going. But once they saw us together, saw our genuine fondness and appreciation for each other, their concerns seemed to melt.

We wanted to do all the right things to prepare for the day we would eventually marry. We exchanged books on relationships that each of us had read. We talked about all the relevant issues and, naturally, sought out pastoral counsel. One of the things I remember well is how God had prepared me—uniquely and specifically—for a wonderful woman like Linda.

Long before I met her I remembered reading a story about widows and the importance of allowing them to talk openly and freely about their deceased spouse. The article went on to relate that it was important for the new man in a widow's life not to be jealous of her former spouse, but to listen to her attentively and help her work through her grief.

One time when we were alone I could tell that Linda was reflecting on the past. Realizing that they were probably not fond memories, I asked her to talk to me about them. Openly and honestly. She was somewhat reluctant at first, but I gently, lovingly insisted that I wanted to know about everything that touched her heart. Even if it was somewhat painful for her, and difficult for me.

She finally started talking—and the tears flowed until she completely broke down. Linda had always been so strong for everybody else, and in her compassion for others she had not allowed herself to complete the all-important cycle of grieving. I told her that from now on her deceased husband, Gary, was to be a part of *our* family.

She was to feel free to speak of him, anytime, anywhere. His picture would be hung in our future home, his presence welcomed as an honored family member. After all, he was the father of her oldest child. I had not come to replace anything that Gary had been in her past life, I was only there to add to her present—and hopefully future—life. That single, loving act brought us even closer together in our hearts.

I remember afternoons when we would cuddle closely together in a wing back chair and ottoman designed for one and talk tenderly to each other until we fell asleep, arm in arm, nestled together like logs in a fireplace. There was great comfort in our togetherness, both physically and emotionally.

Not long after we met I was scheduled—and had already paid—to go on a Caribbean Cruise with the singles group from my church. I would be gone 7 long, lonely days. Coincidentally, Linda had a girlfriend, Linda Bowley, who was living temporarily on the island of Maui, in Hawaii, and Ms. Bowley had long wanted her to come for a week-long visit. So Linda would go west while, at the very same time, I went east.

A born romantic, I carefully planned cards and letters to her so that she would receive one each day while she was in Hawaii. That thoughtfulness blessed her heart. We each had a good time on our separate vacations, but we also realized that we never wanted to be separated that long from one another ever again. She got back before I did, and was able to pick me up at the airport. It was so good to see her, to hold her, to kiss her. I was more in love with her than ever. Fortunately, she felt the same way and we finally set a wedding date for March 3, 1990.

The time until our wedding seemed to drag on and on, but the time we spent together was never wasted. We did projects together, like reviewing her grandmother's eight-millimeter film footage from the 1940s and 50s. We put together the best of those films and had them put onto a videotape for her whole family.

We also mutually decided that there would be no television outside of occasional Christian programming. Our time together was too precious to waste giving attention elsewhere, especially on the "boob tube!" I wanted to know her heart and mind, I wanted to explore her emotions, I wanted to share books, and, most importantly, I wanted to share our growing faith together.

One glorious morning in March, our wedding day finally arrived! Linda wanted a simple service and we agreed upon a west Seattle mansion for hire. Her pastor would perform the ceremony and only immediate family—and her first husband's mother—would be in attendance. We would have a catered meal at the mansion afterward, and then be on our merry way. It was a wonderful day, in every way imaginable. You can see absolute joy on our faces in the wedding pictures, and from their beaming faces it's easy to see that our family agreed.

Finally being married to Linda was like living a dream. She was absolutely the best wife, companion, lover, and friend in every way imaginable. She was independent and competent in so many ways, yet constantly desiring to follow the lead of her husband. We grew closer each and every day.

In March of 1989, I had won a Cadillac from The Arnold Palmer Pennzoil 50th Anniversary contest, but I didn't really need that car, so I sold it back to the dealer. The money came in handy as both Linda and I had always wanted to go to New Zealand and Australia, but had never been able to do so—until now. I would use every bit of leave I had coming from my job and take three entire weeks off. Newly married and blissfully incoherent, we would spend 17 glorious days traveling to the "land down under."

The extended honeymoon trip seemed like a forced march at times, but we were so much alike—both of us were "Type A" personalities, full of energy and ready to go all day—that when evening finally fell, we were more than ready to go to sleep. On that honeymoon I grew to love Linda more than my own life itself.

When I met Linda, she was financially independent and did not have to work anymore. To stay busy, to stay dutiful, to stay faithful, she did volunteer work at her church. In years previous she had been a very active intercessor in prayer, a Bible study teacher, and even a church elder. After we married, she would take advantage of her situation and travel along with me when I went on audit trips.

My audit partner and I would go to a central motel location, check into our separate rooms, and later in the day Linda would come into town. After my workday ended, Linda and I would go out to dinner and have quality time together. On Wednesday evenings we would visit local churches for the evening service. It was always interesting watching how the Lord was served in other towns, other cities, and in this way we would get a larger picture of what was going on in the body of Christ.

For our first wedding anniversary we decided to take an Eastern Caribbean cruise aboard a Holland America ship with a local Christian group we were both active in. The guest list included 12 couples from different parts of the country. Once onboard and settled, we met a delightful older couple, Delbert and Evelyn Lakes of Ohio, who had been married for 50 years!

During the course of that weeklong cruise, we ended up taking them "under our wing." He was legally blind and she was very frail. They were afraid to leave the ship, and so stayed on board the whole time. We made sure they got to the right location for meetings and meals.

They knew we were an answer to their prayers, but it was Linda and I who felt like *we* were entertaining angels. When it was time to leave the ship, we made sure they got on the right bus with their luggage, and then waved them off warmly. A month or so after the trip their daughter, Cathy Charles, from Xenia, Ohio, wrote to us and thanked us for being so good to her parents. She had been very concerned for them before they embarked on their whirlwind journey, and it was a great relief to her to hear what we had done. During the cruise we splurged and got married again by the pastor in our group, Dr. David Jeremiah.

When we first started talking about marriage plans, the subject of children naturally came up. Before Linda entered my life, I did not have any desire for a child—but the desire was stirring in my heart to have one with her. Linda said that about 10 years earlier she had wanted to have another child, but that her husband Gary had not wanted any more. She said that she wanted to put the subject on hold until we had been married at least six months.

But after only about three months into the marriage, Linda felt that God was giving us the "go ahead." We stopped using birth control, but nothing happened. Just when we had all but given up, Linda got pregnant in June of 1991. After hearing that magical news, we were full of excitement and expectation. As the baby grew in her womb I would read Proverbs over and over to the little one—preparing him for the world—and training another soldier for God.

Life was so good, just then. Everyone was so excited for us, so happy for our true love, birth announcement, and good news. We had not one but *two* baby showers. It seemed as though everyone who came into contact with us wanted to be a part of this blessed event. The ladies that Linda knew through exercise and intercessory prayer in Eugene, Oregon came to a shower that her daughter, Kimberly Ann Dunn, and her good friend, Barbara Hunter, put on. In Olympia our church family had a baby shower for us. My sister even let us use her crib. Life was very good.

But it was about to get a whole lot better.

8 *pounds* better, to be exact!

Michael Robert Carey arrived exactly on his due date: March 15, 1992. He weighed 8 pounds even, and was 21 ½ glorious inches long. 10 fingers, 10 toes, skin as pink as a rose bud. He was absolutely, positively, undeniably *perfect*. Linda had planned to have a local anesthetic administered once her labor began in full, but little Michael came so fast—barely twenty minutes after we got to the hospital—that there just wasn't any time.

I coached Linda through the whole delivery and looked right into Michael's eyes when he came out. With the exception of circumcision time—which I was not allowed to observe—I stayed right with him for the entire next week while Linda recuperated. Linda nursed Michael and would do so for the first six months, as our precious son grew from an adorable, wrinkled infant to an adorable, gurgling, handsome baby boy.

Several months later, on June 4, 1992, I awakened from a dead sleep with severe chest pains. It was almost more than I could stand. I could not sleep; I could hardly sit up. Linda insisted on taking me to the emergency room, but the doctors on call could not find a single thing wrong with me. Could it all be in my mind?

Our pastor was contacted and he concurred that this seemed to be a physical manifestation of a strong "spiritual attack." Everyone began praying and three days later the pain was suddenly gone. It was very stressful for Linda: She had already lost one husband to an untimely death. Now she was nearly overwhelmed by this strange and mysterious occurrence in her otherwise healthy new husband. I tried to shrug it off with little or no afterthought.

I wasn't the only one with physical problems: About a month later, in July of 1992, Linda started having severe stomach pains. The doctor told her that it was probably some sort of intestinal flu, because she had been traveling quite frequently with me and eating at different restaurants every other night.

Her diagnosis? Rich food and too many strange beds.

When her symptoms stubbornly persisted, Linda went in for some more tests in October of 1992. Again, the tests were inconclusive, so she was sent to a specialist and, as is often the case in today's medical maze of HMO's and spotty coverage, she was then sent to yet another doctor.

It was now about a week before Christmas when this third doctor called us into his office and gave us the bad news, the *worst* news, a husband and wife can ever hear. In no uncertain terms he informed us that Linda had a large mass of cancer in her colon and that she would need surgery right away. He said that they would have to cut out a section of her large intestine, put in an ostomy (a hole in the wall of her stomach), and that she would have to get radiation treatments and chemotherapy to keep the cancer from coming back once it had been removed.

Suffice it to say, this grim news absolutely shocked us. After my false alarms with chest pains, we were expecting nothing more than a stern warning about cutting down on Linda's travel—not to mention all that greasy carry-out food.

But this? *This?*

How could this *be?* We did not want to believe it. We *couldn't* believe it. We thought, for sure, that there must be some mistake. That was it. That was the solution: We must get a second opinion. We must make sure, absolutely sure, that this was all some big mistake. The kind you hear about on *60 Minutes* or *48 Hours!*

We went in for further CAT scans and x-rays, but it was true. All of it. Every single word. Linda was naturally devastated, but explained that she did not feel comfortable having the surgery just yet. I told her that whatever her decision was, no matter what, I would support her completely and defend her rights 100%.

Instead of the invasive surgery and radiation treatments, she wanted to try some non-invasive measures such as macro-biotic treatments. When we went back to the surgeon who had given us the bad news, Linda told him, "No surgery." He immediately tried to strong arm her with fear and demeaning comments, shocking her with grim statistics and telling her that she was acting out of little more than base fear. Before he got very far I cut him off and said that he had already received the only answer he was going to get. Then we left. It was an emotional and quite difficult decision, but like every other one we had made in our marriage, we had made it together. As a team.

Cancer might have insidiously invaded my wife's body, but it wasn't going to destroy our marriage…

Almost immediately, I changed jobs. In order to spend more time with Linda, to care for her, look out for her, protect her, I took the first job offer I could find where I would not have to travel. It was in training as an Industrial Insurance Claims Manager for the Washington State Department of Labor and Industries. This job was so timely because I had to learn a lot of medical terminology in order to complete my assigned duties. It really helped Linda and I to make the proper medical decisions for ourselves, and not be intimidated by doctors and their ten-dollar words.

I worked hard all day at my new job, and then came home to make carrot juice and herbal tea for Linda. It was all part of her macrobiotic treatment—beating cancer with nature, not plutonium! I would pray for her every chance I got and, the weaker and weaker she got, the more and more I had to care for Michael on my own. Naturally, I enjoyed being home more, spending more time with Linda and Michael. But the strain was growing incredibly tense, and it was getting harder and harder to keep up a brave front for my young, innocent son.

Linda was seeing a local Naturopathic doctor who had been highly recommended to us by a friend, Dick Noel, who had been diagnosed with cancer of the prostate. He later got better with her treatments, and had nothing but glowing praise for the kind of alternative medicine she practiced. And, in due time, Linda also got some good reports from the tests that this doctor made throughout her long and arduous treatment plan. Linda was also losing weight under this strict diet, but from the all-natural foods she was consuming, she had probably never eaten *better.*

In April of 1993 we went to get a healing prayer at a crusade in Phoenix, Arizona from none other than Benny Hinn himself. The healing power of the famous spiritualist lifted Linda's spirits, but in short measure her body hurt even more than ever. It was excruciating to watch her suffer, and many times I prayed to the Lord that we could switch places, that I could be the one getting sicker, while poor Linda only got better. Still, my prayers went unanswered, and Linda continued to deteriorate.

Right before my very eyes…

In May I was getting close to the end of my intensive job training with the Washington State Department of Labor and Industries, but now I needed to be at home more than ever. I requested, and was granted, a half-time position in a job with duties in the same state agency. It was, indeed, a godsend. This part-time job was far less demanding, and now I would only have to work 2 and 1/2 days a week, instead of 5. Obviously, my main concern was not the money—but keeping our medical insurance plan intact in case Linda's condition took a turn for the worse. During the months I was initially in training a couple of friends from church were coming to the house a few times a week to help Linda and keep her company. Now Karen Rogers from our church would come to be with Linda while I was at work. She was such a blessing as she helped with young Michael and gave Linda encouragement.

In June of that year Linda encouraged me to go to a much-anticipated men's retreat, but I said I would only go during the day—and then come home at night. My gut instinct told me that there was no longer any way I could leave Linda home alone for any serious amount of time, let alone an entire 24-hour stretch.

My instinct proved to be dead on…

After the first evening of my doomed men's retreat, I came home and, that very night, Linda got up and passed almost an entire pint of blood through her colon. I told her that I thought we should go to the hospital, but she said she just wanted to lie down for awhile. She said she was all right in the morning, and in the past I had learned to trust her judgment about her own body, but by the end of the next week she was in so much pain she could not stand it anymore.

I immediately took her to the emergency room and the doctor read me the riot act! I just let him have his say, and then asked him to do whatever needed to be done for Linda. There comes a time when self-counsel—let alone self-medication—must inevitably give way to those in the medical profession who wage war with human disease and misery on a daily basis.

This was just such a time…

Our church family gathered around us at the hospital to pray with Linda, but on the following Monday she was forced to undergo surgery. *Radical* surgery. In fact, I honestly think that Linda's operation gave new meaning to the words *radical surgery*: They had to cut an incision from her sternum to her pubic bone, take out about nine inches of her large intestine, remove one ovary, and cut a hole through her abdominal wall for an ostomy opening. This was so her semi-solid waste could be released, four inches off to the left of her belly button, into a plastic bag, called an "ostomy bag."

After this intense operation and invasive procedure, and during the next four weeks, Linda slowly got stronger. The signs were so hopeful, yet I had to force myself to lose the cynicism that had wormed its way around my bitter heart. All of her successes in the past had been followed by some tragedy, but perhaps, just this once, her success would stick around for awhile.

Perhaps…but not likely.

Like many people during this time period of the early 90s, we had an HMO called *Group Health* to cover our extensive medical insurance. This meant that we had to go to see an oncologist some 35 miles away in Tacoma, who would coordinate Linda's cancer care. To fully prepare myself before that initial meeting, I read Linda's medical file from cover to cover. I was disturbed to see that the contents included not only medical findings, facts, and figures, but also a note of personal feelings by the surgeon, who naturally took great exception to our initial decision to put off the radical surgery Linda had just endured by his very hands.

I quickly realized that every doctor who saw her file would also see this letter on the top of her other charts, forms, records, and assorted papers. Not only did reading Linda's medical file help me understand the bias from the medical profession that we had encountered thus far, and were likely to encounter over and over again, but knowing the medical facts of her case would help me know what questions to ask in the future.

In many ways, I felt like I was going to college all over again…

Unlike myself, the Tacoma oncologist had not read any of Linda's medical file prior to our get together. He attempted to bluff his way through the meeting and I immediately called him on his lack of knowledge about her particular case. He admitted he had not read her medical lab reports. I was quickly learning that in modern medicine, perhaps more than any other professional field in the country, the squeaky wheel does, indeed, get the grease!

He would not make that mistake again, nor would I allow any other practitioner to do so, either. Linda's health was too important to let my wife be bullied by doctors long on credentials—and short on attention spans. At times I felt I had to protect her, even from the very practitioners we relied upon for medical care.

Next we had to travel to Seattle, over 60 miles away. There they told us that Linda would have to go to Seattle several times a week for her radiation treatments. There *were* private facilities available in Olympia, but only by referral from Group Health. There was no way I could take all the time required to shuttle her there and back as many times as she needed, because I had to work in order to keep the medical insurance going.

Group Health expected her to take a shuttle bus—on her own—mile after mile, day after day, week after week, dreading the treatments the entire way. We also had a baby that needed constant care. This prospect was naturally intolerable.

The additional strain this would put on her was unacceptable…

I pressed the radiologist hard on the issue, pleading our case and belaboring the long and unnecessary distance we would be forced to travel, and she finally relented: Linda would eventually have her treatments at a closer facility in nearby Olympia.

The daily radiation treatments would be supplemented by chemotherapy, which was given to her in a concentrated form, and her treatments were both intense and unforgiving. She went every single day for a week, and then had three days off to recuperate from the shock to her already delicate and fragile immune system. Linda was becoming weaker and weaker from all the treatments she was getting, and becoming very ill as a result.

Around this same time our church had a visiting evangelist, Dave Roberson, make a welcome appearance on August 5, 1993. Linda was too sick to attend and so a friend, Lori Bjerke, agreed to stay with her while I went. Few events could get me to leave Linda's side these days, but this one was important to me. To *us*.

Evangelist Roberson had a word of knowledge for us regarding Linda's illness, and I was there to receive his prophetic word on her behalf. At one point during the evening, he said she was healed at that very moment.

It was 8:30 p.m. Exactly.

When I had left Linda at the house earlier that evening, she was sick to her stomach and lying feebly in bed. When I got home from hearing Evangelist Roberson speak, she was sitting upright in the family room, talking to Lori and looking quite healthy. I asked Lori what time it was, *exactly*, that Linda began feeling better.

She told me about 8:30 p.m.

Feverishly, I told Linda and Lori what had happened and, more precisely, at exactly what *time* it had occurred. The two women exchanged an odd glance between each other, and then looked back at me. Tears of joy flowed down our grateful faces as we gave thanks for Linda's improvement, but little did we know the battle for Linda's life was just heating up.

Four weeks later, in September of 1993, Linda had to be hospitalized again with severe stomach pains. As had happened so often throughout her various hospitalizations and medical visits, the doctors performed a full battery of every test conceivable, yet none of them could give us a valid reason for her symptoms.

Yet even as Linda was poked and prodded, pricked and pinched, I had my own suspicions regarding the massive radiation treatments she was receiving in Olympia. I was convinced that she was being internally burned by the radiation pummeling her internal organs. What else could explain the fact that her stomach was often the source of her most violent complaints? Eventually, she was released after a couple days and I took her straight home.

Only five weeks later, in October of 1993, Linda had to go into the hospital once again—with the very same symptoms. Yet this hospital visit would be worse than many of the others, if only for a very different reason. While in the hospital, Linda had a headache and asked a nurse for some Tylenol. All we wanted was for the nurse to respond to our simple request.

Instead, the nurse rendered her unwanted opinion: Linda had a headache because the cancer had now spread to the base of her brain. Brain cancer! Diagnosed by a nurse with too much time on her hands, not enough medical school, and no sensitivity to her patient!

We were shocked, and I immediately wished that we had never asked the nurse for anything in the first place! I watched Linda's face, so hopeful that the doctors might be able to find something, *do* something this time, drain of color and turn as ghostly white as the crisp white sheets on her single bed.

That was the last straw. I confronted the nurse, then we angrily contacted our insurer, who immediately sent a patient liaison to hear us out. Thank God this woman was a Christian, so she could understand the futility, the weariness, the exasperation, of our tenuous position. She suggested that I write a letter addressing specific parameters regarding Linda's health care, so that any and all practitioners of medical care could be referred to it in her nearby medical file. This small piece of advice would help considerably in the near future.

When Linda came home from the hospital after this latest, distressing visit, I knew that she was going to need more and more help. Her condition had worsened and I was beginning to recognize the handwriting on the wall just as easily as I could read the lines etched so deeply in her beautiful, pale face.

Concerned that I was not up to the challenge on my own, I talked this issue over with our pastor, Don Nicholson. Many times he had taught his congregation about ministering to one another, so I felt the need to make ourselves available to the rest of the church during this time of great need. We needed not only their task-mastering support, but their prayer support as well.

Even as distressed as I was over Linda's deteriorating condition, it was my fervent wish that we could all grow together in this struggle. As a church. As a community. I told him we could hire someone, a private day nurse or perhaps a live-in aide, or we could give the church an opportunity to be a part of our daily struggle. He welcomed my suggestion and our church family quickly became a Godsend to both Linda and I.

After all that she had been through—the macrobiotics, the radical surgery, the chemotherapy, the radiation, hospital visit after hospital visit, false diagnoses, missed diagnoses, misinformation—the doctors finally admitted that there was nothing more they could do for her. Homebound, her options dwindling with each passing day, Linda was on ever-increasing doses of pain medication as late fall settled over Washington with a misty, gloomy chill.

In fact, her need for ongoing relief was so great that she was on a synthetic pain medication, dispensed continually via a patch placed directly on the mottled skin of her once muscular, athletic back. Unfortunately, it wasn't working very well. The medication would either be too strong, making her woozy and knocking her out altogether, or not strong enough, causing her tremendous pain as she struggled with the rigors of her advancing disease. Despite the patch's inefficiency, it was our only option—short of morphine.

And we knew that to begin using morphine was to abandon all hope...

We would struggle along this rocky path from November of 1993 until January of 1994.

Linda's mother had died some twenty years prior, and Linda had had very little contact with her mother's family ever since. This was mostly due to the fact that she had moved to Oregon a few years after she got married, and had lived there for fifteen years. But Linda had returned to Washington after her husband, Gary, died in a tragic snowmobile accident in January of 1987. Her main purpose in moving back to Washington at that time was to see her family—especially her father, Gus Nelson, and brother, Mike Nelson—receive Jesus as their Savior.

Her grandmother, Bernice Greenleaf, was still alive and so was her mother's sister, Toni. Grandma Greenleaf was in her early 90s, and a bit of a recluse, but otherwise *very* healthy. As Linda's condition worsened and her family could no longer deny the inevitable, we met with them all, as well as Linda's daughter, Kimberly Ann Dunn, in Seattle in December of 1993. For the first time, we were able to get pictures of all four generations: Bernice, Toni, Linda, Michael, and Kimberly.

While the holidays were spent with family and friends, the New Year found us no better off once the tree was taken down and the decorations were back in the attic. By January of 1994, the pain medication Linda was receiving via the inefficient patch on her skin was not managing Linda's pain very well. We went back to the doctor for x-rays around this time, and the results were not good. Not good at all…

The doctor said that there was nothing more to be done, except to go to the next level in pain medication and to get us some hospice care in the home. This would involve a bathing nurse, family on-site counseling, and a nurse to monitor Linda's pain medication needs.

It was the last stretch, the longest yard. We both knew it. The doctor put her on a low dosage of morphine and in the weeks to come this dosage would gradually, little by little, day by day, increase.

As I had discovered was the case with so many other things medical, there was a slight Catch-22 involved: The stronger morphine was working much better than the patch had to manage Linda's pain, but now she was sleeping more and more. Knocked out from the morphine, a shell of her former self in the drug-induced coma, practically hibernating in the painless mist of the powerful painkiller.

The painkiller that was slowly shutting down her organs, one by one…

Death was slowly creeping over this house, this *home*, which was once so filled with hopes and dreams. I could do very little but see to Linda's comfort—and watch as the life began to drain out of the body of my beautiful bride.

I knew the morphine was killing her. Slowly but surely. How much longer did I have with her? How precious were those brief minutes when she was lucid enough and I could talk to her. Despite all the many ways I had tried to prepare myself for her death, I still was not ready to lose her. I don't think I would ever be ready. It hurt too much to think about.

With one last stab at sharing my feelings, I tried to talk to Linda about my concerns for her health, her safety, and, most importantly, her increasing use of, and dependence on, the morphine. But after being in so much pain for so very long, it was obvious to me that she could not even begin to think about cutting back on the amount of morphine she was taking.

I couldn't really blame her. Despite my sleepless nights and moist eyes, I had no earthly idea of the amount of pain Linda was enduring, or *had* endured up to this point. From the violent nausea caused by the chemotherapy to the racking pain in her stomach caused by the radiation, not to mention the ravages of the cancer itself, I knew her days were a living hell, and her morphine-induced nights her only time of sweet relief.

To cope, I tried to busy myself with helping Linda—and taking care of Michael. Still, I couldn't help but be all over the map in my feelings: Sometimes living in denial, even hoping against hope for some kind of a "miracle." Other times I found myself dreading the grimly inevitable, even hoping for her ordeal to finally, inevitably, be over and done with.

Naturally, it was difficult to keep a positive mental attitude with family and friends. Still, I felt that I owed it to them to be upbeat for everyone else, to prop their spirits up, even while, internally, mine sank to the lowest depths of depression and despair.

My heart was daily breaking. I was lonely for my wife, and felt so helpless. Nothing had worked, not the natural therapy, not the chemotherapy, not the evangelist's message or the prayers or the hope or the faith or the love or the desire. I felt so frustrated, so *impotent*. Linda and I had been a ministry team. Yet it seemed as if whatever gifts we were destined to share had all been destroyed—or at least neutralized.

Not only was I losing my beautiful wife, but I was losing my best friend as well. The worst part of Linda's illness, especially this last and brutal phase of sleep and haze, haze and sleep, was that the painkillers that gave her such much-needed relief literally robbed us of our close and loving relationship together.

Never awake for too long at one time, Linda was often incoherent or at the very least "hazy," making the passionate and giving conversations that had been the lifeblood of our marriage something of the far, distant, long-ago past.

Meanwhile, in my 2 and 1/2 days in the workplace I spent most of my time keying in medical-related bills at the Department of Labor & Industries. Despite the menial nature of my part-time job, this was nonetheless a small, welcome respite from the daily ordeal I endured back home. Here I was able to get out of the house, for a little while at least. At work I listened to scripture memory songs to strengthen my much-depleted faith.

During the days scripture was soothing, my pastor was caring, my friends were giving, but the one person I needed to talk to the most—Linda—was all but lost to me in her morphine induced haze of sleepy days and snoring nights. The nights were long on loneliness and short on sleep for me as I listened to the sound of my wife, once so full of life, now so old in form and being sucked into the cruel vortex of death.

A source of great comfort during these trying times was Michael.

And what a comfort he was…

From the very beginning, Linda and I had made a mutual decision *not* to let TV interfere in our daily lives. When Michael came along, we *did* get some inspirational videos of the Animated New Testament for him to enjoy. Now, we watched those videos whenever Linda was awake.

Which wasn't often: She was now sleeping at least 18 to 20 hours per day.

She would wake up to eat a little food so she could take more medication, and then she would drift back to sleep again, leaving Michael and I to sit alone on the couch and watch our inspirational videos together.

One of the videos was "the Good Samaritan." Michael and I watched it over and over again, escaping inside its heartwarming themes and familiar Bible characters. In that video there is a song. It says, "my hands are the Lord's hands, without them how would the world know His touch? I will go where He would go, and do what He would do, so that everyone I meet will know His love."

Linda told me once, long before the pain and sickness and disease and morphine robbed us of adult conversations, that I was the Lord's hands in the way I took such good care of her and Michael. Linda predicted that Michael and I would grow to be the best of friends. But I disagreed: Linda, I felt, possessed the Lord's hands. Not I. She had a very special way of touching with her hands; her caresses of the face were intoxicating and her hugs were inspiring.

I learned from her and, in turn, would make sure that Michael got those same types of touches from his father. Those touches would become a tradition I instituted each night when I tucked Michael in. I would caress his head, his neck, his back, his arms, his legs. He would often say, "touch my head," or "touch my back." In many ways, now more than ever, touching Michael brought just as much comfort to me as it did to him.

Eventually we asked Linda's daughter, Kimberly, and her husband, Philip Dunn, to take our dog, Ritz. He was a delightful pet and it was a tough decision for us all, but we did not have the time to give him the care he needed anymore, so they took him. And we were grateful.

In the weeks to come Linda would need more and more care. The church family would help so much, both morally and spiritually. Four people came over each week to pray with us: Dave and Carol Russell, and Bill and Linda Kelly.

They were a Godsend of strength and encouragement...

By April of 1994, Linda needed a hospital bed, oxygen therapy, and was up to taking 400-500 milligrams of morphine per day. Naturally, her illness had devastated her and she was very weak. Linda's brother, Mike, his girlfriend, Lori Page, Linda's dad, Gus Nelson, and his wife, Virgie, were visiting one day and I took Mike and Gus individually, and Lori and Virgie together, into the den to express to them Linda's desire to see them accept Jesus as Lord and Savior.

I asked them to read Romans 10:9–10 aloud and then asked them if they wanted to receive Jesus into their hearts. Gus, Virgie, and Lori all said "yes." But Mike said he was still not ready. Three weeks later, however, Linda led Mike to the Lord. With this done, a great peace came upon Linda and, for a while at least, she looked happier and more peaceful than I'd seen her in months.

On one of Kimberly Ann's visits, Linda and I sat down with her to share what we knew was the inevitable. Naturally, it was Linda's desire that Kimberly and I remain family after her departure. Kimberly's father, Gary, had died seven years earlier. Now I would be the only father figure left in her life, if she would allow me to, that is. Fortunately, she did. From that day forward I was called "Dad."

It was my honor...

As often as possible, I took Linda to church at the regular meeting times. I had to push her in a wheelchair, bundled up and clutching her portable oxygen canisters. If she got too tired, which was often the case, I took she and Michael home early. Linda came first, all the time, every time. That's just the way it was.

I loved her with all my heart, and to the very end I would be her devoted servant all the way. Many people looked at me during that time and called what I was doing a "sacrifice," but I never saw it as such.

To serve this woman I loved more than my own life was *my* honor.

Linda and I had shared many things in our lifetime—happiness, loss, tears, gladness, joy, compassion, touch, and our wonderful child, Michael. But we had also shared wedding vows that read, "until death do us part." We both took our vows very seriously, and there was nothing I wouldn't do for Linda.

Before, or after, her death...

During the beginning of May 1994, Linda seemed to be getting stronger and no longer needed her oxygen. In fact, she wanted to sleep with me in our bed! Seeing her brief respite as a gift, perhaps a final one, Linda now let people whom she had been keeping her condition a secret from come to visit her. They were understandably shocked at her appearance, and had a hard time trying to understand why Linda had not told them, if for no other reason than that they could have been praying for her.

But it was no secret to the man who knew her best: All her life, Linda felt like she had to be strong for everyone else. Her fight for her life was so great, her struggle with the grim specter of death so difficult, that she did not want to deal with having to prop up the spirits of friends and family. Whether it had been right or wrong in the eyes of others was no longer the point. It was her wish, and I followed her direction as best as I could.

Hurt feelings could always heal.

Linda, we feared, could not...

In the end Linda's strength, her courage, her revival, her grace period, however brief, had been little more than that quiet, peaceful, calm moment during a hurricane known as the "eye of the storm."

By the end of May, she took a tragic and final turn for the worse...

It was clear to me that her time was running out. The doctors had to put her on an intravenous morphine drip, complete with a self-administered pump that could be squeezed, as needed. It was obvious to everyone, perhaps even Linda herself, that this was the final stage of a long, bitter process.

She still wanted to sleep with me in our bed, and I wouldn't have it any other way. In fact, her deteriorating condition all but demanded it: I was sleeping less and less, anyway, not knowing when the end would come and desperately wanting to be there when it did. In the past months, I had to rise several times during the night to give Linda her medicine.

More recently, I had to wake and turn her onto her side several times each night. With her muscle mass disappearing day the day, the bones of Linda's body were pressuring the ever tightening flesh, eventually causing painful bed sores. She was too weak to turn herself over, so I would do what I could to help her be more comfortable.

On June 3, 1994, I told Linda how hard it was for me to see her having to go through so much pain. I told her I knew the end was near, that she was fighting against the inevitable, and that I sensed she was hanging on out of concern for Michael and I.

I did not want her to leave us, but I could not stand to see her suffer…

Calmly and quietly, I told her that Michael and I would be okay. I asked her if she wanted to go home and be with the Lord. Patiently, I waited for her answer.

Finally, I had it: She said, "Yes."

I called her daughter, Kimberly, her father, her brother, and then our pastor, to share with them Linda's decision. They all came to the house. Our pastor served Linda and I our last communion together. Tears welled up inside of me as the full realization hit that this would be the last time we would take communion together.

With all my strength, I refused to break down. I would not make this hard on her. I could not torment her with my tears of sorrow. She seemed stable, and by then it was getting very late. I suggested that her father and brother go home, get some sleep, and then come back in the morning. I told them that I would call them if anything happened.

Kimberly and Philip stayed the night in our guest room. That night I slept about one hour, if that. Instead I listened intently to Linda's breathing, wanting to be there at the end to comfort and encourage her on to the next life. Her heavenly life. I did not want her to feel alone at the end, even though I knew the Lord was with us.

I wanted *my* face to be the last earthly sight she saw…

June 4.

1994.

6:30 a.m.

Linda was awake early that morning. She usually liked to have a little glass of milk for breakfast. It coated her stomach and allowed her to take more medicine. I sat her up and tried to give her a sip, but her morning meal was just not to be. It simply wouldn't go down. The milk just came out of her nose. After being strong for so very long, she was finally so weak.

Linda whispered that she wanted to lay down beside me and just have me hold her. I got her another blanket because her lips were turning blue, and then I lay down beside her with my arms wrapped tightly, but not *too* tightly, around her.

I prayed and prayed for the Lord to take Linda home in peace. Quietly we lay there together in the stillness of dawn. Like a party balloon left in the corner too long after the big day, I could feel the air, the weight, the very *life*, seeping out of Linda's frail and battered body.

With the morning sun light filling our room, Linda raised her arms, let out a breath, and her spirit left her body like a ray of light returning to the sun.

I looked at the clock.

It was 7:30 a.m.

She died with a smile on her face and her eyes wide open. I gently closed her eyes, got up slowly, and quietly told Kimberly that her mom had finally "gone home." I held her in my arms as we cried together. Later we prepared her body for the viewing and her eventual burial.

We washed her body, cleaning it and dressing her in a fresh nightgown. It was only right that we should honor the human body, the earthly vessel, through which God had ministered His love to us and others in so many ways.

It was the honorable thing to do.

As I disconnected all the various equipment that had accumulated in our bedroom, it was all so surreal to me. The tubes, the meters, the dials, the wires. The boxes, the bags, the stands, the crates. Beneath them, Linda lay peacefully, as if she were merely sleeping. As if she were still here. As for myself, I was in a state of shock. I could not feel. I could not think. I could not comprehend the magnitude of what I had just witnessed, what I had just seen and felt.

And now, at long last, my wife had left this earth to join her Heavenly Father.

What would I ever do without her?

I had to keep it together. Take hold of one task at a time. In the tomorrows to come I would forge ahead and do the right thing. Right now I had to be strong for the others who had loved Linda nearly as much as I had. For her family, for her friends. I held them while they sobbed, but I was not able to let it all out of myself. I knew that would come eventually, but for now I merely functioned on auto-pilot.

I asked that the funeral home that would pick up the body respectfully wait until late afternoon so that family and friends from out of town could come to pay their final respects to Linda. The funeral would be closed casket. When they finally did take her body, I asked that they dress Linda in the wedding gown that she had worn four years earlier at our wedding, and that they only refrigerate, not embalm, her body.

By now she had had more than enough chemicals pumped into her body, and I wanted people to remember her as she had been in life: elegant, peaceful, serene, quiet, smiling. Linda before. Not Linda *after*...

A picture of her as a bride would rest on top of her coffin during the funeral.

I would wear the suit and tie that I wore at our wedding.

'Til death do us part...

On June 5, 1994, Kimberly, her husband Philip, and I went to Renton, Washington to make the final arrangements for Linda's funeral. I decided that I wanted to keep Michael away from the funeral service at the cemetery, the memorial service at our church, and all the other ceremonies of grief we adults find so necessary. He was too young to deal with the crying of family, friends, and acquaintances, and I had my hands full as it was.

I also wanted Michael to remember Linda as she was in *life*.

Not as she was…in a coffin.

We picked out a coffin in her favorite color, pink, with her favorite flower, roses, painted on the corners. There were even pearls embroidered on the inside of the lid. I knew she would never know, see, nor even care about such lavish touches, but it was simply another way that I could pay personal tribute to her loving memory. It was a way for me to say to others that "I loved your mother, your daughter, your sister, your friend."

It *wasn't* important. Yet, at the same time, it was *all*-important…

Our pastor, Don Nicholson, would perform the funeral service. Meanwhile, I prepared some of Linda's favorite scriptures, a few personal words for the pastor to share with the audience, and even the music that would be playing softly in the background as mourners arrived. I would also say some words during the service, and I would even be one of the six pallbearers. I could just not seem to let go of being a part of every single detail of the funeral arrangements. Not the music, not the flowers, not even what the pastor himself would say! I realize now that I simply did not want to let go of her.

I had to be a part of it all. Every single moment…

I look back on this experience and wonder what in the world I was thinking. It was too much responsibility to put on one person, but then again my burden of grief was so heavy that the only way I seemed to be able take my mind off of the pain was by being involved in every possible way that I could.

I know that many widowers find themselves inconsolable with grief, drowning in despair and unable to even attend the funeral, let alone be a part of its planning down to the tiniest little detail. But I felt just the opposite…

I was so on the edge, so close to hysteria, that the only way I could keep from breaking down, from falling apart altogether, was to put up a wall of hardness around myself which did not allow for the love of Jesus Christ to shine through. Maybe I *was* taking too much upon myself. God only knows. In the end, I got through it.

In the grand design, I guess that's all that matters…

Linda was buried next to her first husband, Gary Jones, in a beautiful little cemetery in Renton. It was what we had discussed together shortly after we were married: If anything were ever to happen to her, then we both had agreed that that was what I would do. It was an honor to satisfy her final wishes, and my most fervent hope that she could find some solace, some form of comfort, in finding her final resting spot so close to a man she once loved so dearly.

The day after the funeral we had a memorial service at our church so that people could share their grief, precious memories, and favorite songs together. When it came to worship, it was Linda's habit in those times of her greatest joy to sing and dance before the Lord at church. I suddenly remembered Linda at that moment, and I danced in the joy of the Lord—even *with* a broken heart inside. I shared through my tears my undying love for Linda and my endless thankfulness to God for the gift of her in my life.

On the home front, Michael would often go into our bedroom to look for his mother in the days directly following her death. Over and over, day after day, he returned to the one room he knew he could always find her during her lingering illness. Always searching.

Never finding…

He would walk around the bed, even try to climb up on it, his tiny little hands reaching up, ever up, in vain as he endlessly searched for that source of comfort that was gone to him now. Gone to him forever. He would come back several times a day and repeat the entire process all over again. It was as if he was thinking that maybe, just maybe, she might come back to him.

If he just looked hard enough, that is…

Naturally, it broke my heart to see him go through this, time and time again, only to wind up teary eyed—and empty handed. His time with his mother had gradually decreased over the long, lingering months of her illness, but now it was finished altogether. Even more frustrating was the fact that he could not accurately communicate what was going on inside his little, breaking heart.

Instead, he would run and run and *run* all through the house, as if daring his mother's ghost to tell him to stop. One day, from 6 a.m. until 7 p.m., he ran all day long—with only the occasional breaks for meals, drinks, and a brief nap.

It was, literally, a *marathon* of grief…

Now that Linda was gone and the golden temptations of summer were at hand, people came around to the house less and less often. At the memorial, perhaps emboldened by their grief or maybe just for something to say in those painful, quiet moments, folks promised that they would come around "just as much as ever." But, eventually, it all stopped. Our doorbell fell silent. Our living room went empty.

But not quite as empty as our broken hearts...

I took a month off from work to settle Linda's estate and go to Eugene, Oregon to visit Kimberly Ann for two weeks. When I got back home I was going through old medical bills that had piled up over Linda's lingering illness. I was deciding what needed to be saved for our records, and what could be discarded.

Halfway through my chores I made a startling discovery: On **June 4**, 1992 I had suffered an unexplained attack of some sort that the doctors could not diagnose. Two years later to the very day, on **June 4**, 1994 my wife, Linda, had died.

What was that all about? What was the connection? Were Linda and I as connected in death as we were in life? Were my chest pains two years earlier some kind of a *warning*? Was God trying to tell me something?

It remains a mystery to this day...

2

Searching and Hoping

o o o o o o o o o o o o o o o o o o o o o o o o o o o o o o o o o o

Hope deferred makes the heart sick, but when desire comes it is a tree of life.

—Proverbs 13:12

Before Linda died, she told me that after her death I should take some time to find someone who would be a good wife to me—and a good mother to Michael. In the lonely days after she passed away, I thought about her words more and more often as the nights grew long—and more lonely. Finally, and not without some grave reservations, I took action by getting back on the mailing list of the Christian organization through which I had originally met Linda.

Feeling a strong sense of déjà vu, I nonetheless started writing letters and receiving mail in response to my ads. Nothing of real interest had yet come my way, but I was very concerned that whoever I met come with personal references, and I would expect to provide the same. I talked to my pastor about giving me a letter of recommendation should the need arise, and he said it was a very good idea. He was extremely supportive in my first, few tentative steps toward finding a new companion, and his guidance meant the world to me at a very vulnerable time in my life.

Meanwhile, Michael was having a very hard time coping with the loss of his beloved mother—and the day-to-day realities of missing his working father. Since I continued to work half-time, it was imperative that Michael be in daycare while I was gone those 2 and 1/2 days per week.

He cried nearly every minute I was away…

It tore my heart out when I heard this news, and I could picture poor little Michael acting out in the only way he knew how as the world around him changed, inexplicably, forever. First his mother went away, never to return, and now his father had to leave him with strangers nearly three days a week.

"What next?" I could imagine him thinking. "What will happen *next*? Doesn't anybody love me anymore?"

After two weeks I could see that being in daycare at the church was not going to work out for either Michael or myself, so I arranged for my pastor's daughter, Kelleen, to watch Michael at our home for a couple of weeks while other arrangements could be made. Fortunately, just as I was approaching my wit's end, I was approached by a woman at church who offered to take care of Michael in her home. She had three older children and, in addition, did daycare for two other children as well. We gave it a try and, after only two days, Michael was already doing better.

Oh, how a father welcomes such small miracles...

In the meantime, my pastor's wife, Bobbie Nicholson, asked me one fine day how my search for a suitable mate was going. I told her the truth: I had not yet heard from anyone that I particularly wanted to meet. She smiled nonetheless and said that there was someone she and her husband, Don, knew who lived in Albany, Oregon that I might want to contact. Shrugging, I let it go and didn't really think anything of it at the time.

Several days later, however, I suddenly remembered the conversation and I was curious to know why Bobbie had mentioned this woman in Oregon to me. A week later I approached her about the conversation and, in reply, Bobbie simply pulled out a piece of paper with a woman's name, address, and phone number on it. It seemed a better alternative than seeking out another nameless stranger through the endless stream of want ads I'd been writing lately, and I reluctantly decided to give this grown-up dating game one last chance.

I started to write the woman whose contact information was on Bobbie's note and, within the week, I had my first response. I did not know it at the time, but this was no accident: there were "things" going on behind the scenes. Perhaps taking her cue from the meddling old matchmaker in *Fiddler on the Roof*, Bobbie had been startled out of a restful sleep in the middle of the night and the name "Bonnie" had suddenly sprung into her restless mind.

She then woke her husband, my pastor Don, and asked him what he thought. Don told her to talk to Father Horn, Bonnie's pastor. Father Horn and my pastor had known each other for about fifteen years. Our two church groups were in close contact with one another. I had even attended the church in Albany twice with Linda, but had never met this person named "Bonnie" in all that time.

Father Horn knew me as part of the church leadership team, and he also knew Bonnie, thus he initially gave his blessing on our burgeoning correspondence.

Several weeks after this woman named Bonnie and I began writing letters, we talked on the phone and finally agreed to meet. Naturally, I felt I could trust my clergy in regard to her character, so for once in my life I completely let my guard down and opened myself up to our first meeting.

Aside from my, and *her*, pastor's blessing, I realized I didn't know all that much about Bonnie, aside from a few basic facts. For instance, I knew that she was a public school teacher and that she had been married once before when she was 40, if only for about six months. She was almost 44, while I was 45. I knew she had a large family and that her childhood was very difficult.

Other than that, our first date would, indeed, be "blind!"

It all started out auspiciously enough, and just seemed to steam roll from there: I picked Bonnie Joann Vickers up at her millionaire brother's house in Eugene, Oregon. It was an impressive structure and I was duly intimidated. All the while we were making small talk in the doorway, however, I couldn't help but think of poor little Michael. He would stay with his half sister, Kimberly Dunn, while we were out on our "date."

I already missed him…

Bonnie seemed genuine enough to me, in my weakened condition, and so I immediately thought that she was a good candidate for marriage. In retrospect, of course, it is painfully obvious that I was not exactly thinking straight. Still not yet out of the woods as for as the grieving process over Linda was concerned, I simply wanted to get the pain of the past behind me—and get on with life.

Without a lot of forethought *or* planning, I officially asked Bonnie to marry me. She responded positively, if not exactly *passionately*, and we ran the idea by our respective clergy in short order. They both agreed to discuss it with us in the next few weeks, and we made appointments with both couples. Along with their counsel, naturally, they had several concerns and questions.

Their main question was, obviously, "Was it all too *fast*? Was it all too *soon*?"

Bonnie's pastor, Father Horn, voiced his concerns about whether she had told me "everything" about her past and, more importantly, what she had been dealing with in counseling over the previous year. Father Horn did not elaborate on what issues Bonnie was receiving counseling for. In my rush to put the past behind me, I obviously didn't pick up on this "clue."

Nonplussed, Bonnie told them that she had completed "that phase of her life" and that she was, in fact, "healed." When answering such personal questions, I saw for the first time that Bonnie had a demeanor about her that seemed to say, "don't ask; don't question me."

That should have been another red flag, but I was obviously in denial...

Without much fanfare—both of us had been married before—we set a date for the wedding and asked for all four of the clergy who had introduced us to one another, befriended us, *counseled* us, to be in on every aspect of the ceremony.

We also agreed upon how, and more importantly *where*, we would live after we were man and wife. Michael needed me more than I needed to work, so I would stay home and be his primary caregiver in his formative years. Bonnie had a job with the Greater Albany Public School District that she loved, and was not overly fond of long commutes, so we agreed to live in her hometown of Albany, Oregon.

This decision would be step two in what I have since grown to call "the biggest mistake I would ever make." In one fell swoop I would quit my job, sell all of my real estate holdings, and use the proceeds to stay home and raise Michael.

In so doing, I was setting the stage for my eventual downfall: Not only would I relinquish power as the main provider of the family, but I would instead put Bonnie squarely in that coveted role. In turn, this would establish Bonnie, and not myself, as the "dominant" partner in our relationship, giving her just what she needed if, and when, most definitely *when*, our relationship soured and it came time to dispute custody of Michael.

In essence, I gave her all the cards...

Furthermore, I began to pay off all of Bonnie's considerable bills—totaling nearly $37,000—including the purchase of the SUV she was leasing so that there would be no additional payments to burden her as we entered into the holy state of matrimony. She already had a small home, and we would live there temporarily until we could figure out some other arrangement that was mutually beneficial to the three of us: Myself, Bonnie, and Michael. In the meantime, I made some improvements to make the house more livable.

Alas, our little house was destined *never* to be a happy home...

Before the bells even stopped ringing on our wedding day, things began to grow sour between Bonnie and I. Instead of enjoying a weeklong romantic getaway, it became an "invalid's honeymoon" as she continually complained of chronic back problems. Her back went out on her on the second day of our vacation and, from that point forward, seeking massage therapy became the focus of our entire honeymoon.

I lugged the bags and waited on her—Bonnie sat back and complained. When the honeymoon was, quite literally, over and we got back to our normal lives in the real world, Bonnie explained in no uncertain terms that she had a specific daily routine that left very little time for Michael and I.

She left home at 8 a.m. every morning and got back home at 5:30 p.m., although it was often as late as 6:30 or 7 p.m. on Fridays. I could not understand why it took her so long to come home when school got out at 3 p.m. Her fellow teachers would be calling at 4 p.m., looking for her, and incredulous that she was not home yet. What made it even worse was the fact that we lived less than a mile from the school where she taught!

Had she been the principal, or was perhaps coaching an extracurricular soccer team or something, I could have easily understood the long hours and intense dedication. But I had always heard that one of the few perks of being a teacher was at least getting home early!

On those days when she *did* arrive home "early" at 5:30 p.m., she told me that she did not want any "personal interaction" for the first 30 minutes of her homecoming. I was not to ask her any questions, make any requests, or in any other way interact with her at all. Shortly upon returning home she would have an exercise program to complete, and then she religiously watched her taped episode of *General Hospital* before the evening news.

Because of our schedules and his early bedtime, Michael and I were used to eating dinner at 5 p.m. I worked hard to hold him off until 5:30 while I fixed fresh-cooked meals in anticipation of Bonnie's arrival. Yet quite often she would not want to eat just then, or would take her sweet time coming to the table. Meanwhile, Michael was starving. But if we started eating without her because she was dawdling or running late, then she took exception and let us know how "disrespectful" that was toward her.

It was a "lose-lose" situation: My son was hungry and my wife wanted me to show her respect by waiting on her. If it was just me, I could have easily waited, but I could not—and *would* not—try to reason with Michael's hunger pangs.

Meanwhile, little Michael would fall asleep by 7 p.m., so he did not get to see much of Bonnie at all. When I occasionally brought up the subject of her strict after work routine, she simply responded that Michael could "stay up later." However, Michael was getting up at two in the morning and there was no way to get him to change his sleeping schedule at that point.

Or mine...

Naturally, I would get up to be with him for awhile and get him settled in with some toys. I would try to get some more sleep afterward, but was constantly up and down for the rest of the night taking care of him. With such a rigorous and unbending schedule in place, Michael wasn't the only one not seeing a whole lot of Bonnie.

There were other problems with our marriage as well. I did not know anyone in the community other than Bonnie and her contacts. It was very lonely for me in this strange house, in this strange neighborhood, in this strange town. I had little Michael, and he had me. And that was about it.

From the start of our marriage, I noticed several things that made me very uncomfortable. First of all, Bonnie slept with a hunting knife under her pillow. At least until I asked her to stop doing so. She also had two hunting rifles under her side of the bed. She also had a great deal of martial arts training: she was, in fact, one test away from getting her black belt, and she had throwing knives, machetes, and Chinese stars stashed throughout the house. Additionally, she also had two handguns: a .357 and a .38.

Naturally, all of these weapons in the house made me nervous. Not so much for myself, but for poor little Michael. I had never had any reason to own a gun in my life. The last time I shot a firearm was when I was in the U.S. Navy, more than 20 years earlier. That was understandable: The country was at war. But now?

It was somewhat more than strange, and just this side of creepy…

There were other red flags as well: When I would ask her questions about her past, or perhaps why she felt a certain way about something, she would get very defensive. Questions that got too personal would get a sharp response from her: "Are you questioning MY integrity?"

"Why are you demeaning ME?"

"Why are you assassinating MY character?"

Despite my better instincts, I learned to choose my words *very* carefully and step awfully quietly around my new wife. I had heard people use the phrase many times, but I had never before understood what it meant until I experienced it myself: It was exactly like "walking on eggshells."

All the time…

When we were in public or hanging around with church acquaintances, Bonnie seemed to go out of her way to put me down or belittle me in front of others. It was almost as if, no, it was *exactly* as if…she *enjoyed* it. She would tell stories, tall tales, really, about how I had failed at some task or another, or perhaps how I probably wouldn't even bother to give her a hand if she was hanging over a cliff.

At best, these allegations were totally unfounded.

At worst, they hurt my feelings terribly…

I did not like being around her, and grew to dread those undeniably tense moments when she would arrive home and disrupt the peaceful environment Michael and I shared while she was away. Naturally, I wanted our marriage to work. I wanted it, I wanted *us*, to succeed. To survive. To avoid becoming yet another divorce statistic. But more than anything else, I wanted to believe this would all pass…but it wouldn't.

Finally, at ten months into the marriage, perhaps somehow sensing that things were slightly off kilter, Bonnie's pastor, Father Horn, asked to see us to find out how we were doing. Before the meeting, I intended to take full advantage of this opportunity and wrote out what I was seeing, hearing, experiencing, and, most of all, *feeling*.

While we were at the meeting, I asked Father Horn to set me straight if he felt I was out of line in what I had written. Instead, he told me, right there in front of her, "Unfortunately, you are seeing things very clearly. Bonnie is still quite sick. I asked her if she had told you what she had been going through with counseling, but obviously she had not. We have to get you some grief counseling for the loss of Linda, and then worry about Bonnie after that."

Perplexed, and even somewhat vexed, I asked him, "If you knew what her problem was, and what she was dealing with, then why did you allow us to marry?"

He replied, "I saw how strong and stable you had been for Linda, and I was hoping that you would be strong enough to pull Bonnie through her dark issues."

I was flabbergasted, to say the least. As for *her* feelings on the subject, Bonnie was *livid*. She said that I had betrayed her by writing that letter and not letting her see it before we had a counseling session together. She demanded to see it. For my part, I deferred to her pastor, Father Horn, who said, "You do not need to see the letter, because it serves no *purpose* for you to see it."

But Bonnie would not let go of the issue. She was outraged and resented everyone involved over it. I really believe that that moment was truly "the beginning of the end." Still, I did not want to admit that I had been duped or that I had been a fool for rushing into a marriage with someone I hardly knew.

Instead of admitting defeat and breaking things off, I pressed gamely on. I decided to try to make the best of things. I even offered to help her grade papers at night, all in an effort to have more time with her. Well, *that* didn't happen. She could not sit down with me for more than ten or fifteen minutes without jumping up to go do something else. It was not only frustrating, but it wasn't getting us anywhere, either.

I thought that maybe if we could minister to other people together, then we could perhaps work through our own problems. In that vein, we became group leaders for a local marriage ministry group. (Looking back in retrospect, the irony is almost, *almost*, laughable!)

We were supposed to prepare lesson plans together as part of our weekly duties, but Bonnie would either complain about doing so, or just make an outright excuse as to why she couldn't. I would end up preparing most, if not all, of the lessons by myself. In life, I tried to stick to the teachings, which emphasized "not embarrassing your partner." But Bonnie would do just exactly what we were *not* supposed to do. It was very uncomfortable, both for myself and, from all indications, the couples we were supposed to be ministering to!

We had tried counseling off and on together, as well as individually, but that didn't do any good, either. The battle lines were such that the best we could do was have small, trivial truces. I sold my home in Washington State and made plans to build a home that was more suitable for us to live in, i.e. larger so that we could have more space—apart. Bonnie would sell her small home, and the equity would just about pay for landscaping the property and a few decorating expenses.

In my spare time I designed a home, then had an architect draw it to code. I hired a builder, and would eventually pay cash for the construction of the home. *Our* home. It was a lot of work, but at least it would keep me busy enough so that I didn't have to think about the problems we were having in our marriage.

Eventually, the house was finally done and we were trying to get the landscaping completed to put the finishing touches on the house that was to "save our marriage." But instead of joining in on the family togetherness of turning a house into a home, Bonnie was tense and angry most of the time.

One day I looked up at the house I had practically built myself, at the landscaping and decorating I had done, and I have to admit: I just plumb gave up. I had just tried to keep the peace at any cost, financial, emotional, or otherwise. Yet it had little or no effect on Bonnie, *or* our marriage.

After that, I didn't actively care about repairing our relationship anymore. I certainly didn't want to fight with her, but I realized that getting along with her was no longer an option. To top it all off, she was depressed and talking about divorce. If I'd had the sense, I guess I should have just pulled the plug on the marriage right then and there, but I would simply *not* give up.

I tried to just make the best of things by getting involved with volunteer work when my son started preschool. Eventually I would be on three boards of directors, help at his preschool when there were field trips, be involved at the indoor park where I took him several days a week, as well as being involved in the church by leading a weekly men's Bible study, serving on the Church Board, and both establishing *and* leading an ongoing mentoring program!

But staying busy didn't stop our relationship from spiraling out of control. Even in the summertime, when Bonnie did not have to work, she wanted her free time to sleep late and putter around. She was doing a lot of writing, with the hopes of getting a curriculum published. But then, it didn't matter what she was doing, she was quite often too busy to deal with Michael.

I put him in morning daycare at First United Methodist Early Learning Center, where he attended preschool and eventually kindergarten. I also served on the Board of Directors there. At the center, Michael could play with children his own age, and then I would do things with him when I picked him up afterward.

We would go out to lunch, go to the park, and just hang out. On the other hand, I felt that Bonnie's involvement with Michael was "staged." For the most part, she did it to make herself look good in front of others. She was into "her schedule," and that left very little time for Michael in the beginning of our marriage. However, her actions would conveniently change later on in the marriage when it would be more advantageous for her to be seen in the community as "actively involved" with Michael.

Meanwhile, Michael was getting more active and a lot more vocal on the home front. He was beginning to explore his surroundings, check things out physically, and getting harder and harder to keep underfoot. Seeing the handwriting on the wall, and more than my share of needless accidental shootings on the evening news, I bought Bonnie two locking gun cases because I was concerned about safety issues.

In short order, Bonnie "lost" the keys.

By the time she had started making a conscious effort to begin doing things with Michael, the things she was doing really began to bother me. For instance, she would invite him into bed with her and then undress him. Then she would take her own clothes off and hold him close. *Too* close, in my opinion.

I asked Bonnie what she thought she was doing; what that was all about. She told me that the autism specialist at the educational service district said that it was "good bonding therapy." My gut reaction told me that it was sick, and I did not like it one bit. When I questioned her about it, however, she gave me the usual: "Are you questioning MY integrity?"

"Why are you demeaning ME?"

"Why are you assassinating MY character?"

It became like a mantra with her. In the end, I just backed off. She would also take Michael into the shower and have him sit on the counter in the bathtub while she dried her hair naked. When he would get erections, she would invariably point at him and laugh uproariously. I told her that I didn't think her actions were funny *or* healthy. All she got was upset and angry, as usual.

Eventually, I would come to regret not taking firm action on all of these strange behaviors, but, as they say, "hindsight is 20/20."

3

Disconnecting

The thief's purpose is to steal and kill and destroy.

—*John 10:10*

In May of 1997, despite the mounting difficulties in our crumbling union, I decided to try a different tactic to save our marriage and whisked Bonnie away for a weekend getaway to a romantic spot on the scenic Oregon coast. The setting was bucolic, the lodgings indulgent, the scene, as they say, was set.

Yet from the very beginning, it was quite obvious that Bonnie was not "in the mood." Indeed, instead of going through the charade of making excuses or even being the least bit pleasant, she told me in no uncertain terms that she did not enjoy making love to me anymore. Rebuffed again, and perhaps even for the last time, a switch went off inside my heart and I told her just as resolutely that I would not "bother" her anymore with my physical needs.

As I expected, of course, Bonnie had a few physical needs of her own. However, it would be another six months, in November of 1997, before she came to me in the night wanting to have sex with her husband. Naturally, I relented and let her have what she wanted. We were still man and wife, after all, and it was my fervent hope and desire that not only would our physical needs be temporarily satisfied, but that our impromptu romantic interlude was indeed a sign that we were moving closer to satisfying our emotional needs as well.

Again, I was wrong.

Dead wrong…

Despite the fact that it was *she* who approached *me* in the middle of the night, she never talked about our brief interlude afterward and, much to my surprise, or perhaps I should have expected as much by now, she never came back to me wanting any more.

Sadly, that would be the last time Bonnie and I ever had sex as man and wife. Or otherwise, for that matter. Our marriage may have officially been, for lack of a better term, in tact.

But our sex life was, just as officially, over.

Forever…

By the summer of 1998, it was almost as if Bonnie and I were living not only separate vacations, but separate *lives*. From watching television in different rooms to avoiding any meaningful physical contact, we certainly *did* things separately, even when we were together.

In August of 1998, Bonnie finally told me that she did not want any more physical signs of affection from me. None. Whatsoever. In language impossible to misconstrue, she explained that this new edict meant, once and for all, "no more hugs, no more kisses, and definitely no more *flowers*."

I balked at even the last one! I considered myself to be a romantic man, and sending flowers to my wife brought almost as much pleasure to myself as I hoped it did to her. But despite my arguments, she told me that if I ever got a desire to send flowers again that I was to "send them to someone who would appreciate them!"

It was at this same time that Bonnie began receiving what I considered to be "mysterious" telephone calls, both in the morning *and* in the evening, from a man named Dale Silvers. She had known Dale for several years by now, but she insisted that their friendship was simply a "platonic" one. She would eventually have three of his four boys in her class at school, and their relationship grew by degree.

The mother of the Silver's boys had divorced their father many years ago. I never knew all the reasons. Part of it could be seen as economic. Dale seemed to always live right on the edge of bankruptcy, and he had had several "extramarital" relationships between the time I first met him three years earlier. After the last one ended is when he and Bonnie seemed to take up their own form of "special relationship."

Bonnie's contact in their lives went far beyond mere "teaching." She rarely took an interest in the lives of her students outside of class, but she was obviously making an exception in this case. She purposely became a strong female figure in their lives. She would even go so far as to call them Michael's "god brothers," which I resented. Not only because it was simply not true, but because *she* was the one with the relationship with Dales' boys. It bothered me that she was trying to make a family of her choosing.

It would not include me, but it *would* include my son!

Coincidentally, or perhaps *not* so coincidentally, Dale and the boys lived less than two blocks from the school where Bonnie taught, and I finally began to wonder if her later than average arrivals at our home had something to do with her unnaturally close relationship with Dale.

Things got worse, however, not better. Bonnie had invited Dale to church two years earlier, and even back then she would go out of her way to make sure that I sat between she and Dale so that there would be no hint of "impropriety."

Yet, with the rekindling of their relationship, this was all to change.

And not for the better, either…

If things weren't bad enough during that long summer of 1998, they were soon to get far, far worse as the chill fall air descended on our small Oregon town, like so much of the wool that had been pulled over my eyes over the course of my doomed marriage to Bonnie Joann Vickers.

Several months earlier, Bonnie had given up riding to church on Sunday with Michael and I when we went to pray before service began. She would not even be on time for the Sunday service itself. Instead, she would come along forty-five minutes to an hour later than her own husband and her stepson.

When Bonnie finally *did* arrive at church, she would waltz right up the empty aisle and plant herself next to Dale. If I was sitting anywhere *near* Dale, she would squeeze into the pew and scoot her way between us.

By October, Bonnie was sitting with her hand located squarely on Dale's ample thigh!

That's the moment when I finally had enough! One fine Sunday, after she'd waltzed in late, aimed herself squarely in Dale's direction, wheedled her way into an already crowded pew to sit smack dab between us, and gently placed her hand on Dale's thigh, right there in front of me for the whole church to see, I got up and moved away from the both of them.

After church, I would even go so far as to tell our pastor, Ed Sweet, who should have been able to see exactly what was going on in the first place. I also spoke candidly to the couple who were counseling us, Harry and Annie Mason, and who were also right there in the church.

All three of them said that Bonnie's behavior was totally inappropriate. I asked them if they were going to talk to her. They said that they would, but that they were afraid if they confronted her that she would simply leave the church altogether, and then they would not have any influence at all in her life.

I was aghast…

Not only would they not help *me*, but they were powerless to stop *her*!

At the same time, Bonnie began spreading rumors about me to cover her own illicit actions. She told both friends and acquaintances alike that I was "withdrawing" from her entirely and not even "taking care of my husbandly duties in the home." Despite many of their close affiliations with both myself and the church, the folks Bonnie spoke with were eating it up—and I was literally disgusted with the whole lot of them.

I should have filed for divorce right then and there.

But, despite myself, I *still* could not give up…

Partly because of how Bonnie and Dale were carrying on right under their noses, and partly because of how they had chosen to handle, or more appropriately, *ignore*, the situation, I talked to the pastor and told him that I could not be an effective part of leadership in the church anymore.

I eventually pulled out of all of my former leadership responsibilities and, from that point on, merely attended church like most other people that were there. More naive than helpful, the pastor thought that maybe relinquishing all of my former church leadership duties would give me more time to work on the marriage, but instead it only gave me a crushing sense of bleak and crippling loneliness.

For despite the new and shiny life I had so purposefully built for myself, I actually missed Linda more than ever. More than anything, I missed the friendship and love that Linda and I had shared. All I had left was Michael and, occasionally, some part-time work to keep me going. Even what little fellowship I had formerly shared with my church family was slowly slipping away.

Meanwhile, Bonnie's muckraking campaign was reaching new heights or, should I say, *depths*. I found out several months later that one of her claims during this time period of increased mental warfare was that I was having an affair with someone I was working with!

To increase our family income and, perhaps, decrease my foreboding sense of loneliness, I had recently taken a part-time contract position working as a budget analyst for the Corvallis School District. Naturally, I only worked during the daytime hours when Michael was in school.

Bonnie came up with this entirely false allegation after going through my wallet and finding a woman's name and password on a piece of paper. She never even asked me about it. She assumed, falsely, that I was having an affair and wasted no time in spreading rampant rumors that resulted from this supposedly "incriminating" discovery.

I was a temporary worker for the Corvallis, Oregon school district. Naturally, they did not want to go through the time and expense to get me my own access password to their financial database. Instead, the accounting supervisor simply gave me her name and password to use to get into the system. There was nothing more to it.

But, in the hands of a woman like Bonnie, it became "evidence." She was looking for something to take the attention off of her relationship with Dale, and she certainly found "it." In her sick and twisted mind, she had to have something to use as an excuse for *her* behavior.

Perhaps hoping to "catch" me doing something "illicit," one day Bonnie just dropped in on my workplace unannounced. She said nothing, but she certainly *acted* suspicious.

Disgustingly, this is the pervasive mindset she held fast to as our marriage managed to limp along for another year…

In fact, we "celebrated" our fourth wedding anniversary on October 27, 1998. Momentarily forgetting, or perhaps even unconsciously ignoring, Bonnie's "anti-florist" mandate, I had ordered flowers to be sent to her workplace. After that fact, she reminded me *not* to do that and if I had to send them to someone else at her work who would appreciate them. There was a lady there who never got flowers and would indeed enjoy them.

I didn't want to waste the money on unappreciated flowers, so I called the florist and told them to send my carefully designed arrangement to another person at her workplace as she had suggested.

Naturally, this act of attrition resulted in an explosion of revenge that was as devastating as it was obvious. Shortly after my "special delivery," Bonnie began what has been oh so (not) affectionately referred to in my family as her "Email campaign" to family members telling them that I had grown cold and indifferent. In a blizzard of Emails that often went on for pages on end, Bonnie accused me of not doing activities with Michael and otherwise growing cold and distant to her.

Bonnie's ire was further aroused when I would not go with her to her brother's cabin in the mountains. Contrary to the spin she later put on the incident to her family and friends, it wasn't because I didn't want to spend the time with her, I simply hated going up there with her because that meant being with her in the car for a minimum of six hours: three hours going and three more hours on the way back.

She insisted on driving the whole way there and back. She cruised along through winding, twisting, turning roads at speeds that were at least ten miles over the speed limit—and it made me sick. When we would finally get there, the cabin had a fireplace that all but invited the smoke to come right back into the cabin—and that nauseated me, as well.

More often than not we froze as a result of the inefficient heating system, and in fact I had already had pneumonia twice in the previous three years. I did not need to put my health at risk any further. Also, quite often the other people who used the cabin did not pick up after themselves or make needed repairs, so it seemed as though I spent most of my time "on vacation" fixing and cleaning. The entire experience was very unpleasant, and did little to improve our already crumbling state of affairs.

After I refused to join her at her brother's cabin once too often, Bonnie began her vitriol Email writing campaign in earnest. At first my family was receptive to her Emails, and even saw them as "informative." But slowly, surely, Bonnie showed her true colors when she began to lace in "her concerns" about my ability to raise Michael as a dutiful, affectionate, participating father.

In short order all but one—Linda's own daughter, Kimberly Dunn—would begin to see Bonnie for what she was really up to, and would begin rolling their eyes whenever Bonnie's familiar Email address would pop up in their in-box. Then they would quickly delete them, unread, like the rest of the "Spam" that came their way each day.

But not Kimberly…

Over time, it seemed that Kimberly began to relate to Bonnie on several levels. Kimberly had been told that she could not have children, and had eventually taken the appropriate steps to adopt a child of her own. Bonnie wanted to adopt Michael, but I would simply not allow it. Kimberly's husband Philip had just started a mortgage business, and Bonnie's brother was in the upper echelon as far as money circles were concerned in their community. It was a heady combination, and Kimberly soon fell under her "spell."

Of more immediate concerns to the up and coming young couple, perhaps, was the fact that Bonnie was Kimberly and Philip's connection to use of the mountain cabin that I personally loathed, as well as the condo on Maui that belonged to Bonnie's brother.

Both Kimberly *and* Philip had affectionately referred to me as "dad" for the last five years, but now that it was a choice between (my) love and (Bonnie's brother's) money—they would appear to choose money.

In January of 1999, things went from bad to worse. Without so much as an explanation, Bonnie took a class so that she could get a "concealed weapon" permit. This in addition to her already impressive cache of weapons scattered hither and yon throughout the house.

The same house she shared with her husband—and his young son…

In addition to the weapons, not to mention the recent weapons *training*, Bonnie also started acting more and more strange as the New Year dawned. To avoid her altogether, I quietly kept to myself and did even more things with Michael. Yet more and more often, Bonnie began to query me about what would happen to Michael if "something happened to me."

I calmly told her that it was "none of her business," and that I had "everything taken care of." In fact, I informed her, Kimberly had been named executrix of my will after the death of her mother, Linda. Yet instead of solving things, instead of satisfying her curiosity, this information only seemed to stir up the hornet's nest and things quickly became more intense after that discussion.

Gradually, she increased her "behind the scenes" talks to our mutual pastor, Ed Sweet. Much like the former flood of Emails, this was yet another campaign to take the focus off of her—and put it squarely on *me*. Despite the fact that I was by all accounts a loving and devoted father and husband, she continued to claim that I was "detached," and not taking care of my family "responsibilities."

Finally, the inevitable happened…

4

The Deceiver's Agenda

o o o o o o o o o o o o o o o o o o o o o o o o o o o o o o o

Do not steal.

Do not testify falsely against your neighbor.

Do not covet what belongs to your neighbor.

—***Exodus 20:15-17*** *(Commandments 8, 9 and 10)*

Later that spring, Bonnie formally contacted an attorney to ask about her options in a potential divorce settlement. Specifically, she was worried about how it would affect her pocketbook. To her surprise, the lawyer told her that if she let the marriage go on any longer, it might cost her more financially.

Shortly thereafter, her decision was made…

When she finally told me she was filing for divorce, it would not be handled privately, between two adults, in the comfort of their own home. Instead, it would be revealed painfully and embarrassingly in front of our pastor and counselors. Bonnie called a meeting under the guise of trying to work out our difficulties, and instead she "dropped the divorce bomb."

It turns out that not only was the drama thought out to maximum emotional effect, but that the timing was also carefully orchestrated so that she could get this all out in the open—a few days before payday.

This way, she could use her paycheck to set up another bank account and to take over fifteen thousand dollars in money out of the joint account I had (perhaps naively) fully funded when we got married. When we got married, she had no money and thirty-seven thousand dollars in short-term debt, distributed unevenly between credit cards, personal loans, lease payments, etc.

Despite the unfolding drama and back-stabbing bank withdrawals, I did not want the divorce—at first. Yet, inevitably, Bonnie talked me into it. In what was yet another (apparently misunderstood) red flag, Bonnie quickly wanted me to go along with only using *her* attorney.

Then she added insult to injury by showing up with a "friend" who would try to mediate a settlement between us. When all was said and done, Bonnie wanted half of her wages for the time we had been married—and she wanted the equity she got out of the house she sold, *with* interest.

Naturally, I thought that was ridiculous. Not only had I purchased our home with cash, but she had lived with Michael and I, without a house payment and only being responsible for the property taxes, for over four years!

Furthermore, she had no debt. Why? Because *I* had paid it all off. All of it. The credit cards, the personal loans, the lease payments. Everything. On top of that, I had done 95%—or more—of the housework, laundry, shopping, meal preparation, yard work, etc.

I had also performed most of the care of her mother for three years, including shopping, taking her to doctor appointments, cleaning, doing her finances, visiting her two or three times a week when she had finally gone in the nursing home, etc.

Yet despite this unequal division of property, responsibilities, *and* duties, Bonnie would continue to up the ante in her aggressive and evolving demands. To add insult to injury, the bottom line was that she really did not want to move. Amazingly, despite the growing acrimony between us, despite the lies, rumors, gossip, and Emails she had sent accusing me of being less than a husband or a father, her offer was that we would divorce—and all live in the same house.

Bonnie, Michael, and I.

One big, happy family…

Of course, as per Bonnie's stringent stipulations, I would not be allowed to entertain female guests. Naturally, she could do as she pleased. When Michael turned eighteen, we would sell the house and split the proceeds.

Naturally, I said: "No way!"

Yet I suppose I shouldn't have ever been shocked in the first place. After all, that is *exactly* the kind of marriage relationship her mother and stepfather had had for most of their 40-year "marriage" (If you could call it that.). While others saw a devoted married couple, in reality they were two strangers living under the same roof—in a divided house. A house where he took care of things and, from day to day, they really had no relationship with each other to speak of.

Meanwhile, as the divorce proceeded and I dealt, day by day, with the increasingly unstable demands and unwarranted divisions of our estate, Bonnie tried to gain more and more of a visible foothold in Michael's impressionable young life.

Where in previous summers she had eagerly coveted her solitude, she now sought to have Michael more and more to herself. I could see what she was doing, and I did not like it.

I didn't like it one little bit…

In May of 1999, right after filing for divorce, Bonnie asked to take Michael to her brother's cabin for a couple days. While I was hesitant at first, she assured me that the two of them "would not be alone together," because she was going to "meet Kimberly there." Begrudgingly, I gave my permission.

Well, she was half-right: She sure wasn't *alone* with Michael. In fact, I found out two weeks later—when the pictures came back from being developed at the local pharmacy—that Dale Silvers had been there as well! I asked her about Dale's attendance and, for the first time in weeks, she was mute. Dead silent. Coincidentally, the pictures of their cabin rendezvous disappeared without a trace and, quite mysteriously, would never be seen by me again.

Later on, as the battle lines were drawn and our divorce settlement evolved into full-scale, all-out warfare, I would desperately wish that I still had them…

Meanwhile, life moved on—for both of us. About this time, I met a woman named Lisa on the Internet and we would talk via the clicking keyboard quite often each day. I had nothing—and no one—left in the community for a social life anymore, and the Internet gradually became my one and only outlet to the world outside my increasingly chaotic household.

More and more, my own home was an armed camp whenever Bonnie came through the front door. It was hostile territory, not a sanctuary. Bonnie was trying to make it as unpleasant as she could for me, with the hope that I would just leave and she could then claim the house. For all of my earlier mistakes, errors in judgements, and missed "red flags," I would surely *not* do that.

I simply *couldn't*…

I felt like I had been living in hell for nearly two years. By being cut off emotionally, physically, and spiritually from the woman I had married, and even my church life, I had lost much of my identity. My maturity.

My manhood…

This new Internet acquaintance, this woman named Lisa, finally gave me an online outlet to share my feelings, my fears, my hopes, my dreams. I could talk to her, and to other friends I had met on the Internet as well. I had not had any respite in years. Yet, slowly, with Lisa's help, all that changed.

And changed dramatically…

When I found myself with a free weekend in June of 1999, I went to visit Lisa in her hometown in Dallas, Texas. Naturally, I wanted to see if she was as special in person as she was over the Internet—and the phone. It turns out that she was a very nice and attractive young woman. After I returned from our brief encounter, we continued to keep in contact through the usual channels. Besides little Michael, it was the one saving grace in my otherwise bleak and miserable existence.

I would visit with Lisa several more times over the course of my divorce proceedings. While our relationship was a slowly strengthening Internet romance, Bonnie eventually found out all the personal details regarding Lisa's identity. She discovered her name, her address, her Email address, her telephone number, and even her *picture*!

Not surprisingly, Bonnie would use this new information to try to smear my image, my reputation, as the divorce proceedings gradually escalated. But she was not alone.

Now she had a partner.

A partner in *crime*…

Bonnie and Kimberly would call and hang up on Lisa at least ten to twenty times a day. (Ah, the beauty, the evidence, of that great invention called "Caller ID"!) In August of 1999, Kimberly wrote a letter to Lisa filled with rumor, gossip, tall tales, lies, and slanderous allegations against me.

Five months later in the divorce proceedings, the court would ask Kimberly if she had, indeed, written that letter. In a deliberate act that took her from unwitting pawn to willing accomplice, the young girl who had once referred to me so honestly, so affectionately, as "dad" would commit perjury and say that she had not. Three weeks later, however, she would be forced to take the stand and admit to lying about the letter.

She had, indeed, written it.

At Bonnie's behest…

In July of 1999, I talked to Pastor Ed Sweet at his request. He said he had been hearing rumors around the church about me, and was visibly concerned that, perhaps, they might be true. I told him the source of those rumors must be Bonnie, because I was not talking about our troubles to anyone.

And most especially not to those few friends who remained a loyal and faithful part of my dwindling church family. Nodding, our pastor said he would "talk to her." Grateful for the help, I waited—and waited and waited and waited—to hear back from him.

It turned out to be waiting in vain…

Eventually, four weeks passed and I finally asked the pastor if he had talked to Bonnie. He replied that he had been "too busy." Getting the message loud and clear, I told him that Michael and I would be attending church elsewhere until the divorce was final. I explained that the tension between Bonnie and I was simply too distracting during the weekly church services.

He reluctantly agreed and, though I needed it more than ever at that weak moment, I bid goodbye to my church family for the duration...

5

Hell Hath No Fury…

o o o o o o o o o o o o o o o o o o o o o o o o o o o o o o o o o
Then two scoundrels accused him before all the people…so he was dragged outside the city and stoned to death. The city officials then sent word to Jezebel, "Naboth has been stoned to death." When Jezebel heard the news, she said to Ahab, "You know the vineyard Naboth wouldn't sell you? Well, you can have it now! He's dead!"

—I Kings 21:13-16

Meanwhile, Bonnie began making veiled threats that I had better cooperate with she and her attorney—*or else*! I tried to ignore her threats to the best of my ability, but soon her overt—not to mention *criminal*—actions left me no other option. Little did I know that she and Kimberly would break into my private safe and make copies of *everything* they could find there.

In addition to what clearly constituted "breaking and entering," the two "bungling burglars" would also attempt to put their spin on the contents of my safe—which mainly contained legal documents, bank notes, and personal letters between myself and Lisa—and try to smear my name, my personality, and my reputation as best they could.

Fortunately, it *didn't* work…

In August of 1999, Bonnie began acting even more strange than usual. Not only was I concerned about her own sanity, but more importantly, I was becoming more and more concerned for the safety of Michael—and myself.

The anger that was so obviously evident in her eyes, the bizarre accusations she was making all over town, the implied threats, the stealing, the blatant lying—it was clear that it was all building up to a head, and I certainly did NOT want to be around when her wrath exploded on the nearest victim!

In one particularly bizarre incident that truly revealed how far she'd come, Bonnie verbally harassed and harangued me in Michael's direct presence. As Michael and I were leaving the house and getting into the car, she literally started trying to cast demons out of me "in Jesus' name." I simply could not believe her. More importantly, I just wanted to get *away* from her. I told her in no uncertain terms to go look in the mirror and start casting out "demons" from herself!

After this unsettling incident, I immediately contacted my attorney to seek some form of relief from the court for Bonnie's outrageous behavior. She was simply getting too weird for her own good, and especially for Michael's safety. She had two handguns, two rifles, a machete, Chinese throwing stars, martial arts throwing knives, and a large hunting knife that she used to keep under her pillow at night.

While I preferred to handle my own business affairs, this was something that was clearly out of my hands—and squarely in the court's jurisdiction! I was asking the court for relief due to her strange behavior and weaponry. The day before my court appearance for my petition to seek relief, however, her attorney called mine out of the blue and said that she would move out of the house "within a week."

While temporarily elated, our triumph would prove to be short-lived…

A week came and went, and I finally asked Bonnie when, exactly, she was going to begin the long and involved process of leaving the house. For three days I asked and I asked and I asked, trying to pin her down so that Michael and I could have something to look forward to. A relief from her anger, betrayal, and lies.

Instead, she flat-out refused to reply…

Finally, a cryptic letter from her attorney to mine appeared, wherein Bonnie stated that it was no longer in her best "financial interest" to leave the family home. As she had done so often in the past, and would continue doing so often in the *future*, Bonnie reneged on her agreement to leave "within a week."

Instead of the seven days she had promised it would take her to leave the house, it would eventually take six long weeks—another month and a *half*—to get a court date again. I was quickly finding that legal actions were now my only recourse to deal with an increasingly belligerent—and defiant—Bonnie Joann Vickers.

Fortunately, that is when the divorce proceedings were slated to begin as well…

The court took my request under advisement and, in November, months after Bonnie had originally been slated to move out of the house, a judge officially decreed that Bonnie would finally have to move out by the first of December. She would also be allowed to have visitation in the home, since that would be the most comfortable option for Michael.

But even when I "won," I lost: During those home visits, I soon learned, it was *I* who would have to vacate the home. *My* home. For instance, when Bonnie got to see Michael for four hours in the evening, then I could not come home until after 8 p.m., when her visitation had finally ended. And when she got to have a home visitation with him for an entire weekend, then I would have to vacate the home—and stay in a motel—from Friday evening through Sunday afternoon!

As far as I was concerned, it was a "lose-lose" situation…

Bonnie's closest relative, who just happened to be her mother, lived a mere ten miles away from the house we had shared while we were married. On the other hand, *my* closest relatives, my parents, lived nearly 200 miles away!

"What," I continually asked myself during this period, "is *wrong* with this picture?"

Amazingly, this travesty of justice would go on for the next six months, from December of 1999 to June of 2000, until the judge finally issued a decree that would be more fair to the both of us. Supposedly, anyway.

I must admit, I had my doubts…

To further add insult to injury, from the start of the divorce action until Bonnie had to be out of the house, I had been sleeping in the den! Like a visitor in my own home, I was bunking down on the couch in a room otherwise reserved as an "office" or "guest room." Imagine, being a "guest!"

In my own house!

Bonnie had craftily left the majority of her things at the house and was now living with her mother, a mere ten miles away. I had to hand it to her, she took to the winning of the divorce wars like a fish takes to water. After deciding that enough was, finally, *enough*, I decided that I wanted the master bedroom back.

Accordingly, I moved all of her things to the den and mine back into the master bedroom. Where, I felt, they truly belonged. I also put a lock on my bedroom door, because Bonnie had been known to go through my things while I was banned from the house—and she was having visitation with my son.

After her initial visitation period finally concluded at the end of that December, I came home one day to find that my bedroom had obviously been broken into. I couldn't believe it! While I scoured every nook and cranny of the defiled room to determine if anything of mine had been taken, I determined that it was less of a robbery—and more of an *invasion*.

Only two days later, however, I would find out that Bonnie had confiscated some of the innocent documents from my safe and had used them to make some serious allegations—all of them out and out *lies*—of child abuse to the local police department. Fortunately, the police could see straight through her lies and nothing came of the matter, but I was naturally very upset.

In no uncertain terms, I told Bonnie in a letter that any positive thing that she had ever done—or hoped to do—in my life or Michael's life was completely erased by her most recent actions. Not to be outdone, for her part Bonnie took that letter in complaint to the judge, erroneously claiming that people she had showed it to thought it to be a "death threat."

The claim was obviously ludicrous—and the judge knew it.

She threw it out without hesitation…

It continued to hurt me a great deal that Kimberly and Philip Dunn sided with Bonnie, and repeatedly lied along with her, to the local police and even the various court officials. In January of 2000, Kimberly lied about writing a slanderous letter to Lisa Jergins, attacking *my* character. In follow-up court testimony three weeks later in February of 2000, she admitted to committing perjury in her previous testimony.

Even worse, there was still nothing in their demeanor that suggested the animosity toward me would ever end. How could they call me "dad" for more than five years, then suddenly and repeatedly stab me in the back?

I don't know that I will ever really know all the reasons why this turn of events eventually presented itself to me. I do know that Kim did not have a good relationship with her father, nor did Bonnie. Perhaps that is yet another point of connection between Bonnie and Kimberly.

From December of 1999 until June of the following year, on any given weekend, Bonnie would make 30 or more phone calls to my home and leave messages of somewhat questionable sanity on my answering machine. Not only was she becoming a real "noise nuisance," but she was also managing to clog up the answering machine at a time when the house was finally for sale and I needed the recorder to advise me when the house was to be shown.

Formerly, Bonnie's antics had only cost me some much-needed sleep.

Now they could potentially cost me the sale of our house!

As if that weren't enough for her outrageous ego and spiraling behavior, Bonnie would also send letters to harass me verbally—and those letters would arrive on a Friday when my weekend with Michael would begin. Bonnie was in denial about having to move out of the house. She deliberately left most of her possessions in my home as a way of saying: "it's not over." She clearly wanted my house—and my son.

Bonnie also knew how—and when—to push my buttons. She had years of practice, and she seemed to thrive on trying to provoke those she hated. It was painfully obvious that she hoped to get some sort of negative response from me that she might use in the ongoing court sessions.

To that end, she knew by having mail timed for my receipt at the end of the week that it would upset and irritate me enough to put a damper on my ability to relax and have fun with Michael. In hindsight, I believe that she was trying to get me to write something inflammatory in response and send it via the U.S. mail.

I have since learned that a person can claim to be a victim if they "perceive" to have been threatened by something delivered to them in the U.S. mail. I informed my attorney of her actions, but I refused to give her the satisfaction of acknowledging her attempts to provoke me. Besides, my attorney said there was nothing that could be done about her actions anyway.

To add insult to injury, Bonnie also had the recycled trash picked up from my curb the night before it was to be collected, apparently so that she could go through it to try to find any "incriminating" evidence to be used against me in our subsequent court dates or upcoming trial. From copies of police documentation obtained during those very same trials, it appears very likely that she also gained unlawful access to my home after she had moved the last of her things out in June of 2000.

While the news didn't exactly "shock" me, it certainly gave me the chills—especially considering the fact that I had the locks changed on the same day she moved the last of her things out of the house!

From the first time she came to the house to pick up Michael for a week of summer visitation, Bonnie refused to give me her new home address, refused to let me pick Michael up at her home, and refused to let me know what activities he would be involved in for the week.

I found this not only increasingly antagonistic, but potentially dangerous as well. With Michael's condition, I needed to know where he would be—and what he would be doing—at *all* times. Her secrecy went far beyond the bounds of human decency, let alone any kind of "motherly" concern.

When Michael would have problems at school or daycare following a weekend visitation with Bonnie, I would automatically ask her what might have "set him off." It was a natural question for any parent to ask another, and between two reasonable adults could have been handled quite thoughtfully to Michael's benefit.

Bonnie never saw things that way. Instead, she would instantly get very defensive and refuse to discuss the matter with me at all. She also attempted to use her position with the school district to do various things that an ordinary parent would not be allowed to do under the same circumstances.

For instance, one time she apparently told Michael's teacher, Lenore Roberts, and his teacher's aide, April Wilson, to give *her* all of the various information, documents, and files regarding Michael and his schoolwork, and that she would be the one to pass it on to me. April Wilson told me privately that they felt very uncomfortable with the whole situation, and would not comply with her request. April had nothing to lose in telling me this information, since she was planning to leave employment with the district very soon, but the others knew they had to be careful about what they said. They desperately wanted to remain neutral, but they felt torn between the unwritten code of teacher to teacher loyalty and their own common sense. They could see the obvious bond that Michael and I had. Common sense told them that I was truly Michael's only living parent and this woman, who was *not* Michael's birth mother, was no longer even living in the same home with him!

On several other occasions Bonnie would simply stop by Michael's school and pick him up, without my permission, whisking him off to who knows where as I fretted and freaked by the phone waiting for her to return him to me. I dissolved into a full-fledged panic one day when she picked him up within 15 minutes of my dropping him off at his daycare. It just so happened to be the last scheduled day of divorce court in March of 2000. Bonnie and I were scheduled to appear in court at 1 p.m. and I had no idea what was on her mind.

No one at Michael's daycare knew where she had taken him.

I was so afraid for the safety of my son that I called the police to locate a "missing person!" When the police finally found Bonnie, she said that she had "just taken Michael to her teaching classroom" because he was "upset." Yet the staff at Michael's daycare said he was only upset because he wanted to ride his bus to school.

He did not *want* to go with her.

By this time the judge had heard all the testimony she could bear, and did not want to hear another word. She would not even give us a court date for this particular incident. Meanwhile, the police would do nothing either, claiming that this was a "child custody" issue in progress, and way out of their jurisdiction.

When the divorce action began in May of 1999, the state of Oregon divorce guidelines had recently come up with the term "psychological parent." According to the Oregon Revised Statute 109:119, the official definition for this term is:

"Any person, including but not limited to a related or non-related foster parent, stepparent, grandparent or relative by blood or marriage, who has established emotional ties creating a child-parent relationship or an ongoing personal relationship with a child may petition or file a motion for intervention with the court having jurisdiction over the custody, placement, guardianship or wardship of that child, or if no such proceedings are pending, may petition the court for the county in which the child resides, for an order providing for relief."

This differs from nearly every other state in the country. In essence, what boils down from all this legalese is the fact that a parent's full legal rights can be superceded by someone who is not even a *biological* parent.

The term "psychological parent" thus becomes a catch-all for anyone who claims to have a relationship with a child. This should be a red flag for anyone with children who resides in the state of Oregon, or one of several other states following Oregon's lead. Anyone who has any amount of contact with a child may lay claim to the provisions of the law and thereby subrogate the full rights of the parent. This is all done in the name of the state, which is "supposedly" acting in the best interests of the child.

For some time now, Bonnie had insisted that Michael begin calling her "mommy." She would even go so far as to refuse to respond to his requests for food or drink unless he addressed her as such. I was, and had been, Michael's primary caregiver since his mother was hospitalized for the first time in June of 1993. Only when Michael was alone with Bonnie did he rely on her to give him what he needed, just the same as he would rely on a daycare provider or a teacher's aide in school.

There was no doubt in my mind that I was the only person with legal parental status in Michael's life. I was the only one who *should* continue to have legal status. Bonnie did not have any status, other than what she was trying to get via this divorce. No matter what I thought, or what seemed logical, the courts did not agree...

The term "psychological parent" seemed to have come about by way of a Salem, Oregon landmark case called the "Sleeper Case." (Sleeper was the last name of the couple filing for divorce. As in, "Oregon v. Sleeper.") In that landmark case, the recommendation of a Dr. Peter Okulitch was used to not only help solve the matter at hand, but also to arrive at the definition used in the Oregon divorce guidelines, such as those found above.

Bonnie and her attorney would eventually press for the use of this very same doctor in *our* divorce proceedings. In fact, the judge eventually allowed the use of Dr. Okulitch to deliver "expert" testimony on Bonnie's behalf. However, after all her wheeling and dealing to hear his "expert" testimony, the good doctor did not end up seeing things Bonnie's way.

Not at all…

Personally, I believe that the good doctor was afraid to come down completely on one side of this issue or the other, but he finally agreed that in *this* particular case it was in the best interest of Michael to be with me, his biological father.

Privately, however, he told my attorney, Bob McCann, and I that he was convinced that it was not so much in Michael's best interest to have visitation with *Bonnie* as it was in her best interest to have visitation with *Michael.*

I couldn't have agreed with him more…

Dr. Okulitch also raised some concerns about Bonnie's frame of mind and mental health, but made no official recommendations as such to the court. Eventually, Bonnie would attempt to discredit Dr. Okulitch's findings—despite the fact that she had been the one pushing for him in the first place—by using two other so-called "expert" witnesses who had not done any case work and were only reporting on what Bonnie alleged—and what Bonnie and her "partner in crime" Kimberly Dunn had obviously "coached" them to say.

In closing arguments I asked that there be nothing more than "transitional visitation," not a prolonged ad infinitum status. I suggested that this transitional visitation would be a period of no more than one year, with decreasing contact.

It was clearly unreasonable to think that our lives should hinge around Bonnie, of all people. I believed that giving her a psychological parent status borne out of a hostile divorce action was definitely *not* in Michael's best interest. It would be too painful and confusing for Michael to have an ex-stepmother who had already shown so much hatred—to the point of lying and even smearing his own father.

I did not see her attitude changing. Not *ever.*

In the final analysis, however, the judge eventually allowed Bonnie the status of "psychological parent." Unfortunately, this would not be the last time I was ruled against: I would be denied my rights as his only living parent time and again…

When the divorce action began in May of 1999, there was what was commonly referred to as a "two tiered" visitation guideline, meaning "250 miles or less" and "long distance," for Benton County, Oregon, where the divorce proceedings were being conducted. Janet Holcomb, the judge presiding over our divorce, headed the committee for revising the Benton County guidelines to insert another category of visitation—and thereby restriction—to the official guidelines.

There would now be "Tier 1," less than 60 miles, "Tier 2," over 60 miles but no more than 250 miles, and "Tier 3," over 250 miles. These new guidelines were officially scheduled to take effect on March 15, 2000. The testimony in the divorce proceedings concluded one week prior to this effective date, but since a decision would not be rendered by the judge until June, these *new* guidelines would apply. Accordingly, Judge Holcomb ruled that I should not be allowed to move "more than 60 miles away" from Bonnie's residence.

Bonnie continued to put her toe over every line drawn by myself, or that language which was contained within the divorce decree. For instance, she continued to visit my son at his daycare when it was not authorized, or show up at his school to pick him up when it was not authorized.

Interaction with Bonnie became both hostile and contentious. It was always a one way street: When *I* had Michael, Bonnie expected me to tell her what activities we were going to do, where we were going to do them, when we would be back, and how long they would take. Yet when *she* had Michael, she told me that this same kind of information was "none of my business."

Within the content of the divorce decree, Bonnie was ordered to return to me "all copies of specific informational items of a personal nature that had no bearing on the outcome of the divorce decree." The judge agreed to include this stipulation in an obvious effort to diffuse the tension between us, because Bonnie had made it very clear that she was going to continue to use all means available to continue the hostilities she had waged against me in the past.

However, after the judge rendered her decision in June of 2000, Bonnie made no effort whatsoever to comply with this order. In December of 2000, I finally asked my attorney to request the court to hear a complaint of "contempt of court" against Bonnie. I was told that it would take "some time" to get the issue before the court. My attorney was right: The matter was scheduled and rescheduled no less than *three* times while Bonnie tried to figure out a way to counter my action!

It took until March of 2001 before I could finally get a court date in order to take Bonnie in for a contempt hearing. On the prescribed day, Judge Janet Holcomb listened to the complaint, then merely told Bonnie to "try harder to comply." There was no admonishment. No clear direction. Not even a follow up court date was set to resolve the matter once and for all!

I was completely frustrated in this attempt to have returned to me what was rightfully mine, locked in an apparent *Twilight Zone* where the opposite of truth and justice prevailed: the "good guy" suffered, the "bad guy" won. I was naturally in shock and quite angry. I often wondered, "If the judge was not going to enforce *part* of the decree, then why do we go through the pretense of honoring *any* of it at all?"

But life in the *Twilight Zone* continued: In months to come, I would later find out that in January and February of 2001, Bonnie had used her contacts to gain access to my home!

Naturally, I had changed the locks on my door after Bonnie moved the last of her things out of my home more than six months prior, in June of 2000. What led me to conclude that she gained access to my house? It was nothing obvious, like shattered glass or misplaced items or even damage to the home.

Instead, it was a small detail: In a follow-up police report made in April of 2001, she let the name of a particular book that she said I had in my possession slip to the authorities. Yet I had not purchased this book having to do with personal security until January 2001!

So how did Bonnie find out about the book? The only thing I could assume is that she may have used her contacts in the local real estate industry to get into my home when it was for sale and there was a lock box on the door. Naturally, I could not prove any of this in a court of law, but the timing of this particular "discovery" was certainly suspicious.

About the same time that I was taking Bonnie to court for contempt, there was some surprisingly good news dropped in my lap: I finally had a buyer for the house! The deal would close the week after my latest court appearance. I had made arrangements to move within the 60 mile radius allowed to me by the court decree, but I was so disgusted at this point that I personally found it almost impossible to comply with such an arbitrary and unreasonable legal decision.

I found out many months later that on March 20, 2001—before the house papers needed to be signed by her—Bonnie had gone to a different attorney in Corvallis, Oregon to see if there was some way she could legally manipulate the system to her own advantage. Naturally, she did not want Michael and I to move. She liked the level of control she had over our lives, and she was not willing to release that control by letting me sell the house and move out of her "reach."

Not without a fight, anyway...

Meanwhile, Bonnie knew full well that I still had a relationship with Lisa Jergins in Texas. In fact, thanks to her expertise in securing information that was none of her business, she already had Lisa's home address, her phone number, and even her Email address!

Bonnie also had addresses, phone numbers, and Email addresses for my father, my mother, my siblings, other family members and friends. She had all this information long before August of 1999. Along the way she made good use of these contacts with a flurry of Emails to many of these contacts, and more.

Naturally, each electronic message she sent was spun with her own particular version of "reality." Her accomplice, Kimberly Dunn, would make use of these addresses as well. On at least two separate occasions, Kimberly drafted slanderous letters for delivery to my brother *and* to Lisa.

It was literally impossible to escape Bonnie's grasp.

Even after getting divorced…

Lisa couldn't move to Oregon because of the restrictions in *her* recent divorce decree. Yet back in Oregon, I had experienced nothing but grief. After the house was sold and the legal matters were decided, I quit my job, concluded my financial affairs in the city, loaded my truck, picked up Michael from school one day, and headed down the road toward Portland.

I remember thinking to myself as I drove, "Why am I living in this hell? Why continue to put up with this garbage?" I did not stop as I passed the arbitrarily imposed 60-mile point. I kept going through Portland, turned east, and left the state of Oregon.

For good…

I was going to be with Lisa and, to that end, I cut off any and all communication with Bonnie. I thought to myself, "She knows where I am going if I leave the state. She has all the addresses for my friends, family, etc. If she wants to see my son, then let her call. I am sick of her and sick of exposing my son to a woman so filled with mental sickness and hate."

Like the poem says, "I took the road less traveled."

And it certainly *has* made all the difference…

6

Looking for Sanctuary

o o o o o o o o o o o o o o o o o o o o o o o o o o o o o o o o o o
You have been my refuge, a place of safety in the day of distress.

—Psalm 59:16

Before I left Oregon, I had become very disillusioned with the education Michael was receiving. Some of the problems were due to the reduction of funds available from the state for education. I realized that this was not unique to Oregon: Most states had experienced such educational cutbacks of late. However, another part of the overall problem had to do with what appeared to be going on *behind* the scenes within the school district itself.

The Greater Albany School district (GAPS) would like to present themselves as a neutral party when there is a dispute between two natural parents borne out of an ugly and inevitable divorce proceeding. The problem was, this was no ordinary divorce—and this was no ordinary person in the form of Bonnie Vickers. She was a very tenacious individual who had long since been noted by her previous pastor as having an unnatural "willingness to do anything in order to win."

I was the custodial and only living biological parent to my young son Michael. I had both legal and physical custody, as so stated in the recent divorce decree. Meanwhile, Bonnie Joann Vickers was the school district teacher who knew everything—and every*one*. She knew that the unspoken rule of the educators would mandate them getting in step with her. Time and again Bonnie used her lofty position to apply pressure on certain individuals in the Greater Albany School district.

Bonnie would also take it upon herself, without permission from me, of course, to come and remove Michael from school without my prior knowledge. I would not find out about this until days, or even weeks, later. Unfortunately, Michael was not capable of explaining it all to me.

Nor should he have had to…

The worst part of the problem was in the all-important development of Michael's Individual Education Plan, or IEP. For example, in October of 2000 the IEP team at Michael's school agreed with me to allow Michael some special accommodations to make his already challenging academic life a little easier.

Among those accommodations was the use of a calculator and a computer. Michael had had use of both such devices at home for some time now, and I felt it would smooth his adjustment from school to home to retain uniformity in these two items. The IEP team all agreed on a timetable for the implementation of these devices in the classroom for Michael.

Yet as of April 1, 2001 they had done nothing in that regard.

Furthermore, Michael knew all too well how to get himself removed from instructional time that he felt was "boring." He would simply "act up" and his teacher or his teacher's aide would take him on a library tour or for a walk around the grounds. I expressed concern about this disturbing development and brought it up with his IEP team. They agreed to do something about it.

Again, I waited in vain for any changes to be made…

Worse than the education he was *not* getting in public school, however, was the example he was getting on a regular basis from his so-called "psychological parent." For my money, it all boiled down to her mannerisms and her way of using people. Very few people knew the "real" Bonnie Joann Vickers, including the Oregon court officials, because she controlled situations so effectively that they would only hear or see what she wanted them to hear or see.

She refused any form of close examination that would call her various actions—illegal or otherwise—into question. Those who were on or at her peer level, or especially those individuals who were below her own IQ level, she would probe for weaknesses. Then she would exploit those weaknesses to her full benefit. Those who opposed her she would provoke, hoping to get the opposition into doing something foolish or get them to give up in the wake of her relentless animosity.

In dealing with her superiors, Bonnie was the consummate politician: always looking for fresh opportunities to self promote and stage certain situations to her advantage. I could see how she plied those people with "nice talk" to their face, while behind their backs she was caustically critical. If her principal, Pat Monson, and fellow teachers only knew how she frequently talked about *them*, they would be shocked. I did not want my son around that sort of mentality.

This is not what Linda had in mind for her son and mine.

Not by a long-shot…

It wasn't just the way she *treated* people, however, but her manners were also atrocious. When I first met her, I thought she was simply trying to be funny, but in time her rude and obnoxious behavior became something else altogether.

For instance, she would often swallow air and belch—on purpose. She would also blow her nose "farmer style," by holding one nostril closed and forcing air through the other so that the mucous would fly out onto the ground or sidewalks. And she would intentionally slurp her soup as loud as she possibly could.

I know now that this was all for effect. And I wasn't alone: One of her students, coincidentally one of Dale Silver's boys, came to the house one day and he observed her behavior. The student said to her: "At home we were taught that it is not good manners to slurp our soup."

She said: "Soup only tastes good when I eat it this way."

Naturally, I had talked to Bonnie a number of times about these, and other, obnoxious behaviors of hers. Yet she persisted in doing them no matter what I said, or even how often I said it! It was almost as if she took some kind of perverse pleasure in making as big a show as possible about her bad manners in public.

It was painfully clear to me—and to anyone else who was paying attention, including my son—that what she was really saying was that she would do as *she* desired, no matter *who* was adversely affected.

Be they man, woman, or in this case, *child*…

Ironically, she even taught a popular workshop in her public school classroom called, "Please, Pass the Manners!" (Without, obviously, ever referring to the Teacher's Manual for herself!) And while the class itself sounded extremely good on paper, her own behavior was a direct contradiction to what she expected her students to practice on a daily basis. I felt that my son deserved a lot better than the life lessons she was exemplifying.

After all, this was not what Linda had in mind for her son—or mine.

It wasn't even close…

When I finally left Oregon for good, I had decided that I would give Michael the type of education that the current public school system would not, or perhaps *could* not, give him of its own accord. I knew it wasn't enough to blame the public schools, but to improve on them in my own life—and in Michael's.

After all, he certainly had the right to an education that would prepare him for an independent, realistic, and *worthwhile* adulthood, not an education that would prepare him for dependency upon "the system."

While many special education teachers join the profession idealistically and full of new, unique ideas to help their troubled charges, it was my experience that these same teachers were often quickly ground down and burned out by the public school system itself. Therefore, I decided to home school Michael for the entire school year. Or at least what remained of 2001 and throughout 2002.

I knew that Michael was capable of more than the public schools had demanded of him thus far—and I eagerly looked forward to proving it once our studies together started in earnest.

As part of my curriculum, into which I did a serious amount of independent research, I would instruct Michael five full days a week, using a modified 3rd grade curriculum from April of 2001 until the end of July. Then I would use a modified 4th grade curriculum from August thereafter.

Michael would finally learn to use a calculator to help him do computations at his grade level—and beyond. He would learn how to add, subtract, multiply, and divide 8-digit numbers. He would learn how to place decimal points, commas, and even dollar signs.

But I was determined that Michael's instruction not be limited to the more "academic" subjects alone. I wanted him to experience real life, as well as school life. He would learn more practical things as well, like how to count money or make change. Furthermore, he would be expected to complete his individual assignments whether it took him 15 minutes—or an hour.

Or even two…

It was all up to him…

The amount of free time available to him each day would depend upon the choices he made—each day. His *personal* choices. Like all students—and children—everywhere, Michael tested me in many ways during our first few months together as teacher and pupil, father and son.

But he also made great strides under my one-on-one tutelage. It gave me great pride to see "the light go on" in Michael's eyes when he got something, truly *got* something, and I felt the thrill of all good teachers everywhere when their students are, in fact, finally learning!

Unlike his frustrated special education teachers, I was free to follow my instincts and let Michael help me lead him where he needed to go. No bureaucracy, no red tape, no IEP forms, no in-services or conferences or faculty meetings.

Just good old-fashioned *teaching*…

When it was playtime—for every school, even *home* school, needs recess—we would often go swimming together, much like we had when he was younger. I remember how he would climb up on my back with his arms around my neck and I would swim across the pool doing the breaststroke.

The candid pictures, the family snapshots, that were taken of us during that time period, and the videotape we made together one sunny Texas day, replay in my mind over and over again as I tend to look back upon that bonding period in our lives together as father and son.

Especially in light of what was soon to happen that would tear us apart…

When we moved to Plano, Texas together after that fateful court decision only weeks earlier, I officially took Lisa Jergins to be my wife. It was a natural move for us—as mature adults, as best friends, as lovers—and one that we naturally discussed at great length before finally committing to. Lisa's two beautiful children, Shannon and Derrick, were amazingly only one year older—and one year younger—than Michael, who was by now nine years old.

From being an only child for as long as he could remember, young Michael was now a "middle" child…

For the very first time, he now had a stepbrother and a stepsister to play with. He finally had other children to open presents with on Christmas morning, help him blow out the candles on his birthday, and wish him goodnight in our own little version of *The Waltons!*

Though I knew our time together as father and son was an important part of his life, and one that both of us truly valued on a daily basis, I was greatly relieved to know that now he would have interaction with children his own age as well. Amazingly, our union as husband and wife, mother and father, brother and sister, molded together seamlessly in the weeks and months after our marriage.

It was all that I had ever wanted.

It was *more* than I could have hoped for…

With my home school duties and other commitments firmly in place, I was also the house-husband in our happy little home of five. As Michael would accompany me throughout my daily routine, he slowly learned how to shop for the things we needed by going with me to the store—and even how to care for a home by doing things with me like cooking, cleaning, and decorating.

I didn't consider these activities extracurricular. I considered them valuable "life lessons" for that inevitable day when I was no longer around to take care of him.

On Sundays the five of us would all go to church together—as a family. Unlike his new brother and sister, however, Michael did not want to go to children's class or Sunday school. Instead, he preferred to stay close to me.

To *us*…

Very often during praise and worship, he would cling to my arm and rest his head against my side as he sang along with the rest of the congregation, his sweet little voice joining together with ours as it rose effortlessly in song, rising and ris-ing...straight up to heaven.

His little dimples, feathery blond hair, and playful laugh reminded so much of his mother, Linda. The resemblance was sometimes painfully similar. So many times in church I would look at Michael and remember the day on which Linda and I had dedicated him to the Lord. Tears would well up in my eyes and I would hold them back so Michael would not see me cry.

Linda and I often shared our plans and hopes and dreams for little Michael's life in the months, weeks, and even days before she finally passed away. In those quiet, thoughtful moments, she often said that Michael and I would be the best of friends as he eventually grew up.

Her prophetic statement was finally coming true...

It had been seven long years since Linda's untimely death. The profound sad-ness I felt in her dying was less pointed now, but still very much present in my daily life. I tried my best to love my son in the ways that both his parents would have wanted for him. I would *talk* to Michael the way Linda had talked to him. *Look* at him the way Linda had looked at him. *Touch* him like she touched him, gently caressing his head and back in the sensitive way she always had. It helped me be closer to Michael, brought Linda back into his life, and helped Michael grow closer to both of us in the process.

I loved my son fiercely and, though it was indeed a financial sacrifice to liter-ally take myself out of the workplace in what was surely the *prime* of my earning life, it was nonetheless such a blessing to share life with Michael that the experi-ence was truly "priceless" in my mind.

To see little Michael grow, to watch him learn, play, talk, walk, run, skip, jump, and laugh are all precious memories that I would come to cherish ever more over the coming years, turbulent as they might eventually become—painful as they had already been.

I didn't yet realize that this was the calm before the storm.

Nor how soon the storm would quickly come...

There was literally nothing I could achieve in my work, no professional honor that I could win, no amount of money that I could earn, no promotion, no 401-K plan, no fringe benefit, no employee perk that could ever mean more to me than to see my son growing strong in the principles of faith. The strong and undying faith that his mother and I had shared when we were man and wife.

Together we had our daily routine, which gave Michael the structure, sched-ule, and sense of order he so desperately needed each and every day. A daily routine that he could count on, religiously, day in and day out, and he was finally thriving in that environment of educational stability and family commitment.

It was no mystery, just simple math: Time+commitment+routine+caring+order+compassion+love=success!

However, I also came to believe quite firmly—and still do—that a large part of the reason why Michael was doing so well at his new home in Texas had to do with the fact that he had finally been separated from an environment so filled with animosity and tension back home in Oregon.

How sad it was to know that to lift him *up*, I had to take him *away…*

My ex-wife Bonnie literally thrived on emotional adversity, and played the "torment game" continually with the family, friends, and even acquaintances that truly did not know the "real" Bonnie.

We were all strangers to her, and that's exactly how she liked it…

Day after day, week after week, weekend after weekend, year after year—she kept us all on emotional edge. Never knowing what to expect, never knowing where to turn, never knowing what might happen next, never considering the face behind the veil might not be the one we hoped to see. I had seen the weaker ones want to believe her or not want to incur her wrath for questioning her actions.

I had hoped in our leaving Bonnie far, far behind that Michael and I could find some peace of mind and a healthy environment together. I had hoped that "out of sight, out of mind" would actually *mean* something to my vindictive ex-wife. I had hoped that, finally, the worst was far behind us.

Little did I know that Bonnie was playing out her most insidious plot to date. Nor that I was to play its leading role…

7

No Holds Barred

o o o o o o o o o o o o o o o o o o o o o o o o o o o o o o o o o

These are people who are given an enormous amount of power over somebody else and they routinely abuse that power.

—**Dr. Melvin Guyer,** *Professor of Psychiatry at the University of Michigan and a practicing attorney*

While I happily began my new life with Lisa and the kids in Texas, events were taking place back in Oregon that I had no knowledge about—nor would I for many months to come. The wheels of justice, make that "injustice," were slowly turning, and Bonnie was definitely in the driver's seat!

First, she claimed to the local authorities that I had committed a "crime" by driving my son to be with his new family in Texas. Yet on April 6, 2001, the Albany Police Department told Bonnie that her complaint regarding my leaving Oregon State was a *civil* matter—and not a criminal one. The documentation and testimony later given in court indicates that Bonnie went to her attorney, Pam Hediger, who used to work in the Benton County District Attorney's office. She put Bonnie in contact with Scott Heiser, the Benton County DA, who assigned the situation to Dan Armstrong, a deputy Benton County DA. Bonnie was referred to Captain McClain of the Albany, Oregon Police Department who directed an officer to take her police report on April 9, 2001. In her report Bonnie stated that I had interfered with *her* custody of *my* son, Michael. The Albany Police were previously directed by the Benton County DA's office to fax the report back to the DA's office so they could get the ball rolling.

By divorce decree, I had physical and legal custody of my son. We did not have joint custody. Bonnie only had visitation rights. On the police report she said that she was the person reporting the crime. So how could *she* be a *victim?*

She also claimed that Michael's address and phone number were the same as *her* address and phone number. Wrong again: *His* last Albany address was the same as his *father's* last Albany address: 1450 NW Patrick Lane. And the phone number for both Michael *and* his father was 541-926-6453.

Bonnie furthermore claimed that *Michael* was the victim. Yet how can Michael be a victim when he was in the legal and physical custody of his own *father?* As it turned out, things only got worse from there, because Bonnie Vickers had to keep on perpetuating "the lie" in order to get her desired end result, which was custody of Michael. In order to get what she never had in the first place, she had to lie and be convincing enough so that the authorities would be forced to believe those very same lies.

Bonnie wasn't acting alone. Testimony during the divorce proceedings in January of 2000 revealed that Bonnie and her accomplice, Kimberly Dunn, acquired the name, address, telephone number, and Email address of Lisa Jergins, who was now my wife. Under testimony, Kimberly Dunn first denied, then three weeks later under oath in court, admitted writing and mailing a slanderous letter to Lisa in August of 1999.

On several occasions during the divorce proceedings in court, and in statements submitted to the court, Bonnie and her attorney of record, Gary Norman, made reference to the fact that they knew of my relationship to Lisa Jergins and conveyed their belief that I would be moving to Texas to marry Lisa Jergins.

And, while Bonnie hired a private investigator around this time to learn of my whereabouts, it seemed like she and Kimberly Dunn were doing plenty of "amateur sleuthing" on their own: Kimberly Dunn's Email to Bonnie's private investigator, Jeff Wilson, dated April 10, 2001, stated the addresses, phone numbers, and Email addresses for my father, brothers, one of my daughters, cousins, etc.

Meanwhile, it seemed that both women knew that they were skirting justice with their slanderous lies and guerrilla tactics. Another Email from Kimberly Dunn to Jeff Wilson, this one dated April 11, 2001, quoted from Ms. Vickers' own journal: "Robert has legal custody, therefore, it is not technically custodial interference."

A copy of the private investigator's files revealed that on April 13, 2001, Jeff Wilson in Eugene, Oregon contracted with yet another private investigator in Dallas to locate me. Progress notes for the month of April, 2001, revealed that the Dallas private investigator had obtained Lisa Jergins' work phone number, home phone number, and addresses for both.

He also had Lisa's Email address and her ex husband's contact address, phone numbers and Email address. The private investigator also had addresses, phone numbers, and Email addresses for nearly *all* of my family members, cousins, and some friends from my church affiliation in Olympia, Washington.

It was startling to witness evidence of the depth and breadth of their investigation into my new life—and incredibly frightening. I was also amazed by the accuracy of the information they were getting.

They were also closing in…

In yet another Email to her private investigator, this one dated April 14, 2001, Kimberly Dunn revealed Lisa Jergins' current address, previous address, cell phone number, home phone number, Email addresses, employer, employer address, phone number, husband's name, his address, phone number, and Email addresses. The Email further stated, quite accurately, I might add: "the Email address that Robert was using with her shows no Email from her for the past week. My hunch is that they are together (no need for Email)."

In an Email dated two days later, Kimberly Dunn told Jeff Wilson: "It is very important, especially until those legal papers are issued, that nothing be done down in Texas that will tip Robert or Lisa off."

Tip us off to *what*?

I would find out, but not for several months. Private Investigator Jeff Wilson's April 18, 2001, investigation status report revealed my family and friends' addresses, phone numbers, and Email addresses, as well as a considerable amount of financial information on myself. The report also stated: "photographs of Robert Carey and Michael Carey have been sent to Dallas, Texas."

The results from their own investigation were truly staggering, and the outcome would be no less shocking: Ms. Vickers went to the grand jury to testify, and from that testimony a warrant for my arrest was issued on April 23, 2001.

That warrant itself stated that "Ms. Vickers had a valid joint custody order and that taking my son, Michael, was a class B felony." Furthermore, the second charge—contempt of court—stated that I "knowingly violated a joint custody order." Yet the divorce decree did not contain a joint custody order.

The divorce decree, recorded on August, 28, 2000, clearly stated that "full legal and physical custody is awarded to Robert D. Carey, Jr." There can only be joint custody if it is agreed upon by *both* parties. That *certainly* did not happen! The judge in that case had to decide who had custody—and it was Robert D. Carey, Jr., *not* Bonnie Joann Vickers.

On May 3, 2001, I made a withdrawal of funds from my account in the amount of $8,000 at a Wells Fargo Bank in North Dallas, Texas. On the very same day as my withdrawal of funds in Dallas, Bonnie's attorney, Pam Hediger, met with private investigator Jeff Wilson for one hour regarding information on my whereabouts.

On May 3, 2001 private investigator Wilson's man in Dallas, Texas had noted Lisa Jergins' address as 3304 Lanarc Drive, Plano, Texas and her employer's address in Dallas, Texas. He also made a brief observation of our home, without sighting Michael or I. All of the address and telephone information was given to PI Jeff Wilson by Kimberly Dunn on March 14, 2001. The report by the PI in Dallas was only to confirm what was already known.

As a result of that action, the District Attorney then subpoenaed my bank records on May 4, 2001, which revealed my mailing address as 7900 W. Shelton-Matlock Road, Shelton, Washington. The Benton County District Attorney received this information by fax on May 8, 2001. This would be one full day before Bonnie and her attorney signed affidavits. They knew that in order to get their desired end they would have to lie about not being able to reach me—and so they did.

It would appear that Ms. Hediger had access to a wealth of information between May 3, 2001 and May 8, 2001, showing that I was in Dallas, Texas and that my mailing address was in Shelton, Washington. Private investigator Wilson, Kimberly Dunn, Bonnie Vickers and now her legal counsel, Ms. Hediger, all had access to the names, addresses, phone numbers, and Email addresses of other family members, friends, and Lisa Jergins.

Bonnie's attorney, Pam Hediger, signed an affidavit dated May 9, 2001 in which Ms. Hediger stated that personal mail could not be delivered to me because I did not leave a forwarding address. Yet the post office had a forwarding address beginning April 2, 2001. Contact with all utility companies for the home I sold in Albany before departing would have revealed my forwarding address, which was my father's address: 7900 W. Shelton-Matlock Road, Shelton, Washington. Furthermore, the subpoena of my bank records on May 4, 2001 also revealed that address.

Bonnie Joann Vickers' affidavit, dated May 9, 2001, stated that she "diligently attempted to locate me" and sent a letter to my former address, but that that letter was returned to her. She claimed to have used "due diligence" in her attempts to contact me, but all the while she had names, telephone numbers, addresses, and Email addresses for me, my parents, siblings, Lisa Jergins, and friends. She did not use any of those means to contact me.

With both of these notarized affidavits in hand, Bonnie's attorney took these documents before a judge and the following was done: The "Order Allowing Service by Publication" was signed on May 9, 2001. Then the "Publication of a

Summons" was made in the *Idaho Statesman* on May 12, May 19, May 26, and June 2 of 2001. Also, the "Publication of a Summons" was made in the *Corvallis Gazette-Times* on May 14, May 21, May 28, and June 4 of 2001.

I have never lived in Idaho. My only connection to Idaho was when I dropped off a rental truck there on April 4, 2001 and picked up another one the same day. I do not have any friends or relatives in the state of Idaho. When I lived in Oregon I lived in Albany. The only newspaper that was read while I was in residence there was the *Albany Democrat Herald*. I worked in Albany and anyone that I had any measure of contact with when I left Oregon lived in Albany. All of this was known to Bonnie. After all, she had rifled through my files, broken into my safe, used contacts to spy in my home, and now had used a private investigator to confirm what she knew.

Several days prior to signing her affidavit dated May 9, 2001 saying she did not know where I had gone, Bonnie and Kimberly Dunn made airline reservations to fly to Dallas on May 20, 2001. They arrived at Dallas-Fort Worth airport at approximately noon on May 20, 2001.

Then they drove twenty-five miles north to lodge at the Holiday Inn Express in Plano, Texas. This hotel is four miles due west from where Michael and I lived in Plano, Texas. The charge for the hotel was dated May 21, 2001. They left sometime thereafter and flew out of Dallas-Fort Worth airport at 5:55 a.m. on May 23, 2001. In a Dallas-Fort Worth metroplex of more than 6 million people, Bonnie took lodging within four miles of where I was living with my son, Michael, my wife, and stepchildren.

Coincidence? I think not...

In an Email dated May 15, 2001. Kimberly Dunn stated that my father, Robert Carey Sr. and Lisa Jergins were the two most likely people to be connected to me. They knew where I was, but they did not want me to know what they were up to. They did not send letters to me, or anyone I knew, for that matter. They did not send me Emails or call on the telephone even though they had my telephone number. They did not stop by the house when they were in the street right in front of our home. They did not want me to know anything regarding a change of custody hearing, because it better served their purposes if I was completely in the dark.

Bonnie's attorney, Pam Hediger, filed a motion for default dated June 18, 2001. At that point, Ms. Hediger had had access to my forwarding address for more than six weeks prior. She met with PI Jeff Wilson prior to this motion on May 3, 2001. Bonnie had traveled to Plano, Texas four weeks prior to this motion. With all this information known to them, Bonnie Vickers and her attorney, Pam Hediger, continued to execute their insidious plan.

Without my prior knowledge, on July 23, 2001, Bonnie's attorney got one of the Benton County Circuit Court Judges to issue a default judgement giving Bonnie both legal and physical custody of my son, Michael. They got a judge who did not hear the divorce case while the judge who did, Judge Holcomb, was apparently on vacation. The judge who signed the order based his action on Attorney Hediger and Bonnie Vickers' affidavits that they had used due diligence to contact me, and that I had defaulted.

At the end of July someone began contacting my Internet friends via Email addresses under the pseudonym Candace "Candy" Cane. Bonnie Vickers and Kimberly Dunn could only have garnered the Email addresses when they entered my locked safe and took information from my computer between August and October of 1999. Ms. Vickers also broke the lock to access my bedroom in December of 1999, when she was at my home having an unsupervised visit with my son.

By order of the court I was not present during her visits with Michael, in my own home. In that apparent break-in she got the Email address for an old friend, Karen Rogers, from my church family in Olympia, Washington, who helped take care of Michael and Linda during her illness.

The Emails that this not-so-mysterious "Candy Cane" sent related concern for Michael's being abducted by his own father, directed recipients to the www.MissingKids.com web page, and actively solicited information from anyone having information on our whereabouts.

It was now the beginning of August, 2001, and I was still not aware of any legal actions that had been going on back in Oregon. I received Emails from friends advising me of the Internet poster and its contents. I viewed the information and upon noting the obvious content errors I wrote and mailed letters to the Albany Police *and* the Benton County District Attorney in an effort to point out the fallacy of the information posted on the www.MissingKids.com poster. I did not receive a response from either agency.

With Bonnie Vickers pushing and former FBI agent turned private investigator Jeff Wilson assisting, the FBI finally got involved by tacking on a "flight to avoid prosecution" warrant. This was predicated on the charge of custodial interference, and, in effect, sealed my doom…

8

In Custody

I've seen children who've been removed from their families by SCF for long periods of time. They're ruined, just ruined. They can't trust their parents to defend them…It's evil, and it's wrong.

—**Velma Hartwig,** *Grandmother and long-time family advocate*

October 9, 2001 started out like any other day in our pleasant little Texas household. None of us had even the slightest hint—not the faintest inkling—that it would be the worst day of our lives, or that it might possibly be our last day together for months, if not years, to come!

Getting three kids ready for school, two off to public school, Michael for home school, was no easy chore, but I for one welcomed the routine, bustle, chaos, and overall *happiness* of my new family life. After being through so much heartache in my troubled life, I had finally learned to take the little things in stride—and to always remember to enjoy life's simple pleasures.

Looking back, that morning was one of the best in recent memory…

Once things had finally settled down, Michael and I did his structured lesson plans from 9 a.m. to 3 p.m., with a few stolen minutes here and there taken off for our built-in snack, stretch, or potty breaks.

After "school," I picked up Michael's step-siblings, Derrick and Shannon, and then we came straight home to continue the just-as-hectic second half of my day. Shannon and Derrick did their homework dutifully at the nearby kitchen table while I began fixing dinner for our happy little family. In the picturesque Norman Rockwell moment, none of us noticed the three cars careening to a stop mere feet away on our quiet, residential street.

Nor could we have really done anything about it if we had…

The doorbell rang at 4:30 p.m. and, naturally, the kids thought it was one of their friends from across the street and rushed from their chairs in a symphony of, "I'll get it!" They fought over who would do the honors, before Shannon finally broke away triumphantly and swung the front door wide open. Instead, the man at the door told Shannon that he was the electrician here to "make a repair."

As the hairs on the back of my neck stood up instantly with the instinct only a father of three could ever relate to, I quickly told my impressionable young step-daughter that no one had been called to repair *anything,* let alone anything of an electrical nature, and to just close the door.

NOW!

Too late...

Instead, the man at the door pushed his way inside the sanctity, the *privacy,* of our residential home and ran straight into the kitchen where I stood, making dinner for my family. In a move I was sure had been well rehearsed back at police the training academy, the large man grabbed me, turned me around, and handcuffed me before I even knew what had happened.

Within seconds, several other men swarmed into the house from all directions by way of the patio door and back entrance. Amazingly enough, the first man identified himself as a detective—a *detective*—with the Plano Police Department. He told me that I was being arrested.

Arrested—for kidnapping.

Kidnapping...

I was in shock. Pure, unadulterated, blanched face shock. The chaotic scene in our once peaceful kitchen seemed to be playing out like something straight from a movie, as if all of this was really happening to someone *else.*

I was unceremoniously wrestled into a nearby kitchen chair while the burly, uniformed men regrouped, rounding up the children in an uneasy circle and checking out each room of the house to see if anyone else might have been hiding in a closet—or under a bed.

I told these men, these intruders, that I had both legal *and* physical custody of my son, Michael, and that I was the only living biological parent that the boy had left in this world. I told them that the person who was behind all of this, who had set this wild and wacky wheel in motion was my ex wife, Bonnie. I calmly explained that she was also the ex-stepmother of poor Michael and that she had obviously told some major lies back in some Oregon courtroom to set all of *this* in motion.

Naturally, the police standing around awkwardly in my kitchen, steam still rising from the stove as they stood, knew nothing about any of our personal—and sordid—history, and said that they were only doing what they had been ordered to do, on the basis of an outstanding warrant.

Trying not to panic now that things had settled down and the unpleasant reality of the situation became all-too-apparent, I asked for permission for my stepdaughter, Shannon, to be allowed to call her mother. The men begrudgingly allowed her to do so, although I assumed that they weren't bound by any law to make that provision.

Meanwhile, I calmly talked to my son, Michael. Routine was what he favored, similarity was what he cherished. A disruption like this could be disastrous to the recent advances we had made in his demeanor, his state of mind, his education.

As plainly, and as calmly, as I could under the circumstances, I told him that this would probably take a little while to get straightened out, but that I would try to make that happen as soon as possible.

"Daddy will be home as soon as he can," I remember saying quite clearly.

Michael came to me and put his arms around my neck and gave me a big hug. I told him that I loved him, and wished for all the world that I could just erase all of the pain and heartache that I had brought into his world, however unknowingly, in the form of one Bonnie Joanne Vickers.

What I wouldn't have given to turn back the hands of time at that moment…

I then talked to Shannon and Derrick. I explained to them about what was going on, reassuring them that everything was going to be all right, that it was all a misunderstanding, that the courts in Texas would work with the courts in Oregon and work everything out.

Soon…

Unfortunately, the police would not allow me to wait until my wife, Lisa, got home from work. Although her arrival could happen at any moment, the police remained firm in their conviction that it was time for me to "leave the premises." Those officers left behind would wait for her arrival and meanwhile I would be hauled out to the awaiting police car in front of the neighbors like a common criminal.

A petty thug…

Three police cars in front of our home, lights flashing like carnival rides as evening fell over our sleepy little street, drew a lot of attention. All of it unwanted. To make matters worse, I was dressed in sandals, walking shorts, and a T-shirt. The outside temperature was in the 80's.

The back of the car did not have car seats, like they always seemed to do in movies. Instead, what I found to sit on was little more than a solid plastic tray—with no seat belts.

("Isn't that against the law?" I can recall thinking quite clearly.)

There was a metal grid between myself and the driver, and I was very uncomfortable because the handcuffs were so tight around my rather large wrists. I am also long legged, so I could not sit for any amount of time without the cuffs cutting into the small of my back.

Meanwhile, I was still partly in denial that all this could be happening to me. It was one thing to watch cops show up one someone else's door—usually on TV—with dogs barking in the background, the sirens flashing, the officers yelling, guns drawn, adrenaline flowing.

But it was quite another to wear the cuffs on your *own* wrists...

I had always lived honorably, thriving as a law-abiding citizen in "the land of the FREE." I had even served my country, and served it well, in armed conflict—and was discharged honorably.

Why was this happening to me?

It all felt like some horrible nightmare, a waking dream—one where I was being taken against my will, forced behind enemy lines, banished into occupied territory, held for ransom, unable to speak on my own behalf.

Memories of being transported to boot camp after I had joined the US Navy began to run through my mind as I sat in the back of that cramped police car and pondered my own, tenuous fate. Back then, I would be told exactly what to do and when and how and *why* to do it.

My current situation didn't feel any different. I was at the mercy of these men, this police cruiser, these handcuffs. If I had been in a movie, perhaps, I would have squeezed out of my cuffs—or even picked them wide open with a spare paper clip that just happened to be resting at the bottom of my back pocket! Stolen the car, broken through the barricades, escaped to parts unknown.

But in the real world, a man has responsibilities. And duties. And an example to lead for his son. In the real world, you don't leave your loved ones behind. To question your motives, ponder your guilt. In the real world, a man—a *good* man—takes his medicine and fights for what's right. Stands up for his beliefs, and works to be proven innocent in a court of law.

In the real world, things always manage to work themselves out.

They just take a little time...

There is something ominous that happens to an innocent man as he's driven—handcuffed and wedged into the back of a patrol car—on his way to the city jail. And not just driven to any city jail, in any nameless, faceless town.

But to the city jail in his very own hometown...

To the same industrial strength building of steel and cement that he's passed by unnoticing, time and time again, on his way to work, or to pay a traffic ticket, or to drop off an old recliner at the city dump. To the ugly city building where everyone in town knows that they house hardened criminals, petty thieves, low-life thugs, and dangerous convicts.

Inch by inch, foot by foot, mile by mile, he is slowly but surely degraded, humiliated, and outraged…

His sense of justice is imperceptibly warped, his belief in right and wrong damaged beyond repair. The world he's come to know and trust, *his* world, is stripped from him as surely as his freedom is about to be upon his very arrival. It feels like a rape, a robbery, a mugging, a home invasion, or some other violent crime that changes him for the rest of his natural life.

And not for the better…

You can live your life as a decent man, a hardworking man, a good man, a *Christian* man—and none of it matters. Not one bit. You can shout it to the roof-tops how you've obeyed the law, paid the IRS in full, parked in all the right spaces, settled all your debts, written endless thank you and get well and Christ-mas cards, and no one—not a single soul—will listen to you.

Not while you're wearing those handcuffs, anyway…

You can pick up litter where others toss it on the ground as casually as blowing their nose. You can turn your library books in on time—*every* time. You can recy-cle, and donate to charities, and put the proper postage on every piece of mail you've ever sent. You can smile and compliment and listen to others, you can let others cut in line in front of you and put dollar bills instead of quarters into the Salvation Army's Santa buckets all December long.

You can return wallets to the lost and found department, instead of pilfering the cash inside and simply throwing them away. You can volunteer at your church, tithe 15 % instead of 10, and try with all of your heart to walk in Jesus' very own footsteps, though all around you 9 out of 10 folks are walking the devil's footpath. You can obey the speed limit, pay your taxes, love your wife, raise your son right, and still be found "guilty until proven innocent."

How many endless reruns of *Justice Files* or *48 Hours* or *American's Most Wanted* or *Cops* had I watched where some simple-minded criminal or drug-crazed nitwit had escaped the strong grip of justice through sheer stupidity, or a clerical error, or a processing mistake, or some other trivial little oversight that left him free to rape, maim, beat, rob, or kill over and over again?

How many drug dealers or child molesters or bank robbers had been let out on bond before the handcuff impressions on their wrists were even gone? How many plea bargains had been met, day after day, before lunch was over? How many hardened criminals roamed free because of overcrowded jails, inexperienced court-appointed lawyers, or lazy judges?

And yet there I sat, hunched over and handcuffed, because I had done what was best—in my own eyes, and in the eyes of the Lord—for my only son? Because I had obeyed a higher law to bring my son where his needs would be met, instead of my ex-wife's? Where he would be the most nurtured, the most loved, the most educated, the most cared for?

These questions I asked myself, over and over, as I was driven—powerless, pitiful, and prostate—in the crowded and uncomfortable backseat of that generic squad car on my way to meet my uncertain fate: Where was the *justice*?

Where was the righteousness? Where was the truth and the honor countless veterans had fought for over the years, the decades, the *centuries*? Where was the sense of freedom, liberty, and equality I had trained for, believed in, and fought for in the US Navy?

What price had I paid for this lack of justice?

And what would it mean to me in the immediate future?

As we slowly approached the Plano City jail, the rigid metal underground receiving doors opened and then closed behind us with a shuddering lurch. It felt like I was entering a deep, unforgiving tomb.

A tomb that had buried my sense of right and wrong, my sense of fair play, my belief in truth, justice, and the American way. Dark and boundless, sullen and morbid—the tomb easily swallowed me without complaint, yet made my escape as impossible as it was unlikely.

Freedom was outside the tomb.

Inside there was nothing but confinement…

Inside the bustling and inhospitable station house I was unceremoniously told to undress for inspection. Self-conscious yet servile, I was quickly strip searched, showered, and told to dress in the standard prisoners garb. The material of the orange jumpsuit was stiff and cold—cheap, new material that had never been washed.

Once the frenzy of my intake procedure was complete and my overwhelming fear, shame, and adrenaline died down to a more manageable level, I found that I was getting chilled in the badly ventilated police station.

Despite the fact that we were completely indoors, apparently safe from the elements and inclement weather outside, I had on no socks, no underwear, only a two piece rough cotton jumpsuit that was more like cotton duck, a light canvas sailcloth, than proper clothing fit for man or beast.

The officer at the processing desk eventually asked me why I was brought in. I told him my story, just like I had told all the others—whether they had asked me or not. This man, this *stranger*, was incredulous.

He repeatedly asked me about the various and sundry details of "the kidnapping." I told him quite simply that there *was* no kidnapping. That this was all a big misunderstanding, a huge lie, and that I was being held on a false charge propagated by my bitter ex-wife.

It suddenly dawned on me that what I was saying was all-too-true. I had been framed, set up, betrayed by a woman who had once been my wife. Who had taken a vow to love, honor, and cherish me—until death do us part. Yet now she was pulling my strings from hundreds of miles away, tossing me into jail for who knew how long with the simple filing of a complaint, with a simple lie and a signature.

How could anyone be so *cruel?*

His incredulity not withstanding, the processing officer was in no position to help me out of my current predicament, and eventually handed me over to the next phase of my incarceration. There, I was fingerprinted and my official mug shots were taken: "Stand here! Turn left! Turn right! Stand still!"

Finally, an alert jailhouse official reached down and held up the back of my prisoner's shirt and noticed the long, fresh cut that stretched diagonally across the lower part of my back. They asked what that was from and I told them that the cut in my back had been made by the handcuffs—about which I had duly complained throughout my long car ride—during transport.

They took a picture to cover themselves in case I filed a lawsuit.

Eventually, I was given my one and only phone call. (Just like in the movies.) Naturally, I called my wife, Lisa, who was very shaken but trying to hold things together there on the home front. The pain in her voice was as audible as the effort it must have taken her not to sound frightened. She was trying so hard to be strong for me, to keep the fear and dread and worry out of her voice. It meant the world to me, and I believe I told her so.

But in the rush of words that we shared in those few emotion-packed moments, I'm quite sure it got lost in the shuffle…

After asking about my situation and seeing that I was all right, for the time being, anyway, I begged Lisa to tell me what had happened on the home front. The news was far from encouraging: By this time the local Department of Child Protective Services had taken Michael away from us—and as of yet we did not know where that would be.

In fact, it could have been anywhere…

Despite the gravity of my own situation, multiple questions about poor little Michael's fate flooded my already overloaded brain: Would he be put in a foster home? Would he be taken to an orphanage? Would he be put in a group home? A detention center for children? Juveniles?

I had heard horror stories (haven't we all?) about such places. Abusive foster parents far worse than those the child had been taken away from. Homes where abuse was as common as head lice and junk food. Juvenile detention centers where older boys preyed on the younger ones like wolves in the hen house.

God only knew what that confused, scared, and mixed-up little boy might have been feeling at that very moment. My concern for him—as was Lisa's and the entire rest of the family's—was literally overwhelming. The pain was nearly impossible to bear. It was one thing to be separated from your son.

It was quite another to have him ripped from your arms…

Poor Michael's plight shadowed every thought and dogged us persistently throughout that long first day and until we all saw him again. Even on good days, in ideal situations, Michael's grasp on reality—not to mention his sense of emotional peace and tranquility—was tenuous. Who knows what he was going through without a single solitary family member to turn to in his desperate time of need?

Shakily, Lisa told me that she had at least managed to help little Michael pack some much-needed items before he'd been taken away from our house. But not knowing how long he would be gone, she hadn't known exactly how much—or even what—to send him off with.

Fortunately, he ended up taking his favorite stuffed animals, some summer weight clothes, his favorite blanket, and his Gameboy video game. It was small comfort, but the only such comfort we had. Lisa and the rest of the family were at least able to give him one final hug and reassure him before he was taken from them.

It was excruciating to be locked up, behind bars, incarcerated for who knew how much longer and to know with all my heart that for the very first time in his young, impressionable life, I could not be there to help Michael with this incredible transition—and it was tearing my heart in pieces.

How could my ex-wife be so cruel, so heartless, so *selfish*? It was obvious to everyone involved that her actions were as far from being in Michael's best interests as was humanly possible, and yet she had managed to dupe an entire legal system into thinking that she was the grieving, dutiful, dependable parent.

Mentally, I railed against this country that I lived in. That I, a loving and devoted father who had done nothing but surround his only son with a new mother and two loving step-siblings, could be treated like a common criminal on little more than the word of a woman—a madwoman—was nearly impossible to comprehend.

If it weren't for the bars in front of me, I wouldn't have believed it myself!

Yet those were the facts. And this was my reality. I was a prisoner. Accused, arrested, apprehended, arraigned, and incarcerated. Outside was freedom, inside was hell. And where was I? On the inside.

All because of one woman's active imagination, superiority complex, and grand illusions about herself, her position, and her importance to the rest of the world. Happily playing out her charade as the grieving mother, my ex-wife had managed to send a truly loving father to jail. With what proof? With what evidence?

On what *grounds*?!?

There was nothing left for me to do but wait for my arraignment and see what needed to be done to get released.

And then *do* it…

In the meantime, my life as *America's Most Wanted* father continued to play out in a very real and inescapable manner. I was put in a holding cell with three other men. The cell was a claustrophobic 11-feet x 11-feet, little more than a small child's bedroom in a single-family home.

For four grown men!

The stifling cell had three drab concrete walls while the wall facing the central booking area was constructed of thick, reinforced glass. The lights were always on, both in the hall and in the cell, yet there was no light from the heavens in this underground arena of musty dankness. The setting reminded me of a pet shop where the animals are put in glassed-in cages along the walls. You can see their every move, on display for any voyeur who might happen to pass by unannounced.

Behind a three-foot retaining wall in the back of the cell was a stainless steel commode and a sink. There were four vinyl-covered pads on the floor that were sleeping bag sized: two-feet by six-feet and about three-inches thick. They were side by side on the floor, creating something akin to a small wrestling mat.

At that point in my incarceration I did not even have a blanket to cover up with—and it was freezing cold. It may have been 75 degrees outside, but inside our own personal tomb it felt like it was below 50. That's what it is like when you don't have socks on your feet, aren't wearing any underwear, and are under a lot of stress.

All I could do was sit, stand, or lie there waiting for whatever came next…

Time moved so slowly, it almost seemed to stand still. Cell mates were coming and going like they were in a turnstile, while I remained the one true constant in our tiny cell for four. One would make bail and leave, and soon enough another prisoner came to take his place. To pass the time I would cautiously try to engage in conversation. Among those with whom I talked I found that most of them were detained for outstanding traffic warrants.

How exciting that I was the only alleged felon in "the big house!"

As the restless evening wore on, prison officials brought us each a small TV dinner that was lukewarm at best. After our unsatisfying dinner, the four of us waited for several hours before we were brought out to the front desk in the underground arena where we would be officially arraigned. I had witnessed the scene played out in hundreds of TV shows and movies, yet to experience it for myself was as shocking as it was humiliating. I waited patiently with my "cell mates" until my case was finally called.

The judge on duty somberly read the very serious charges against me. While they were completely bogus, I knew that disputing them would be completely ridiculous. After all, the judges and lawyers and other prison officials simply had to follow the legal steps on up the chain of command. They did not know the whole truth. They only knew what Oregon had told them—and Oregon only knew what Bonnie Vickers had claimed was the truth.

If it was at all possible, the news I received was *worse* than I'd imagined...

I was told that there were not one but in fact *two* outstanding warrants for my arrest: One was on behalf of Benton County, Oregon pertaining to a charge of "Kidnapping," while the second was an FBI warrant for a crime known as "Flight to Avoid Prosecution."

When finally given the chance to unburden my mouth—and my mind—of the truth, I told the judge in no uncertain terms that I fully understood they had paperwork on their desks testifying to that effect, but I also told them both charges were undeniably false.

But all my conviction did me no good in the end.

After all, doesn't *everyone* in jail claim to be innocent?

After the charges against me had been read, they put me in yet another holding cell with 10 different men. Despite the increase in occupants, that cell was not much bigger than the one they had me in with only three men: 10-feet x 20-feet. Another walk-in closet, admittedly bigger this time, yet now holding far more prisoners per square foot than the first!

To see us through the long, chilly night, we had each been issued a rough blanket and a sleeping pad, or mat. No pillow, no sheets, no mattress, no creature comforts beyond those which were the most base and demeaning. On TV I'd seen stories of so-called "country club" prisons where inmates were all but pampered.

Apparently no film crew had ever been to this city jail...

There were only 4 bunks in the crowded cell, so that meant that most of us were sleeping on the floor for the duration. Despite the pad and the blanket, we might as well have been lying on the cold, hard concrete.

The cement floor, cinder block walls, and reinforced glass cage pet store window were as *chilling* as they were, quite literally, cold. It was cold in the cell and cold on the floor and cold everywhere you turned, and we were told not to cover our heads so that the guards could keep count of us—and monitor our condition.

Needless to say, the night was long, cold, and troubling. I was helpless, restless, and tormented—not just for myself, but even more so for the unknown factors of what poor little Michael was dealing with.

All alone, scared, tired, hurting inside, confused, sad—and lonely...

I was naturally—and rightfully—angry, but it served no purpose to be angry in my present condition. There was no one I could yell at, no one I could berate, no one I could share my pain and suffering with who might reasonably be counted on to help me.

It didn't matter that some of them—or, perhaps even *most* of them—were guilty of the crimes for which they had been arrested. When you're sleeping on the ground with nine other men, you form a bond that is hard to sever. Still, it was apparent to me that everyone in that cramped and crowded cell had their own problems to deal with.

Some of my cell mates never said a single word. They had a look about them that made me not even want to know why they were there. As I compared notes with the talkative ones in the cell, they were incredulous about my situation. They had never heard of such a thing. Most of them knew they had outstanding warrants for traffic infractions, and weren't surprised when the law finally "caught up" with them. It would simply be a matter of hours or at the most a few days until they would be released.

I had no idea of what I was facing—or for how long.

I would find no solace that night.

There was nothing left to do but to trust God...

Still, my faith was sorely tested that long, cold night. I tossed and turned and tossed some more. I slept fitfully, if at all. It didn't help that one of the other prisoners snored so loudly that the rest of us could simply not sleep. I gave up sometime just before dawn, and lay there shivering.

Shivering and praying…

In the harsh light of morning the jailhouse trustee brought each of us a luke-warm cup of coffee or water, a stale sweet roll, and a banana. It felt strange eating industrial-type food served to us by a total stranger, as if I was back aboard a ship in the navy and eating in the galley, or mess decks, as they were called.

If only things could be as simple as they were back then…

After breakfast, there would be another arraignment in front of another judge before I was finally and officially transported from the Plano City Jail to the Collin County Jail. This time I was told that the new charge against me was now something called "Custodial Interference." Despite the somewhat whimsical title, it was a serious charge: a Class B felony.

Meanwhile, the FBI warrant was still pending…

After hours of additional waiting in the sterile holding area, jail officials lined us up, put us back into our street clothes, and put a restraint belt on each of us. This was the most humiliating experience to date: Like Hannibal Lecter, they shackled our ankles and connected our handcuffs to the belts. I half expected that cumbersome hockey mask to materialize next, but fortunately it didn't.

We shuffled out the door—as if we were headed to the electric chair—and escorted up into the waiting van. Thank heaven for small favors: the heater was on. Despite the fact that I was riding in a prison van on the way to an even more secure correctional facility, I was surprisingly grateful: This was the first time I had felt warm in the last 18 hours!

Upon arrival at the Collin County Jail, we were transported into yet another awaiting tomb. This time we would be held in a waiting area for more than 12 hours. After the almost luxurious accommodations in the prison van, now I was so cold I shivered the entire time.

12 long, shivering hours…

After half-a-day spent waiting for the "privilege," we went through the entire process all over again: pictures, fingerprints, information, and a full recounting of the charges pending against us.

Because my warrants came from out of state, I was turned over to a deputy—Officer Linda Cartledge, who dealt specifically with matters related to extradition. Naturally, I told her of my situation and she immediately asked if I had some kind of documentation to support my story. I told her that as soon as I had the opportunity I would call my wife and have her bring it all in.

Meanwhile, I was quickly learning the ins and outs of "prison life." In fact, I wasn't in prison yet. My first stay had been in a station house, meant for short-term prisoners. Now I was officially in a "jail," the halfway house between freedom and long-term incarceration, which happened in a prison.

Between heaven and hell, I was literally in purgatory…

There was no cafeteria in the jail. To have a tray of food, twenty of us at a time would be taken into a holding cell with benches, and locked in while we ate. The quarters were cramped, the food miserable, but I expected no less. After our meal, it was right back out to wait in the cold main room for processing.

At every turn I was exhausted, cold, and miserable…

The entire experience reminded me of boot camp, where expertly trained drill sergeants would tear you down to the basest level humanly possible. The process was designed to take away your individuality and make you conform to the generic system of regulated existence. The only freedom you had was between your ears—and that was where most of it would have to stay.

After dinner they made us take another shower and then change clothes again. In the final stages of our hours-long intake procedure, we had to have a health screening and TB vaccination. The nurses on staff looked at the oversized wound on my back, but in the end did not bother to put anything on it. At that point, I didn't even care. I was so tired. I just wanted to sleep.

And sleep and sleep and sleep…

It was after midnight before we were all marched to our detention wing and put in our sleeping cells. I wound up in a room that was wedge shaped: 4-feet wide at the front, 8-feet wide at the back, and 12-feet deep.

Unlike earlier in the detention process, now we each had a bunk to ourselves. I took the lower one, preferring to stay as close to the ground as was humanly possible. We each had two blankets made of loose woven cotton. It soon became apparent why one was not sufficient: They barely kept the cold off, and I continued to remain chilly all the time.

The only time I could get the least bit warm was when I got under the hot water in the shower—or when I could hold a hot cup of tea in my trembling hands. I had one hotel travel size bar of soap, one disposable toothbrush, and a very small amount of toothpaste. I had no shampoo or shaving gear for the entire time I was there and, having been a fastidious man "on the outside," the grime and grit on my face and hair quickly drove me to distraction.

After another fitful night's sleep in our new surroundings, the next morning started off with the main guard yelling at us like new recruits. He was in every respect just like the drill instructors I had known in boot camp. Everything was regimented and timed. Every detail had to be addressed.

Every "i" dotted, every "t" crossed…

Like other forms of mass instruction—elementary school, boot camp—the infraction of one inmate would result in punishment to all. Few of us wanted to break the many rules intentionally, but occasionally it was simply unavoidable. There were so many rules, and our new surroundings were so confusing, sometimes you broke a rule you didn't even know existed. Punishment usually meant being placed in something known as "lock down," where we were confined to our cells for the duration, which could go as long as 23 hours in a given day.

For our use, there was a bank of six pay telephones. Those phones were our one—and only—link to the outside world. Although on the surface it may sound like a lot, we had to share those six phones between no less than 80 men!

We could only make "collect" calls—with a 10-minute maximum—and they were *very* expensive. Despite the inconvenience, the hassle, and the expense, I tried to call home every chance I got, if only to hear my wife's voice, to reassure her that I was okay, and to get the required documentation to the authorities at the jail for my release.

And, of course, to ask about Michael...

Unfortunately, Lisa did not have any new information for me about Michael. It was frustrating, to say the least, but I did my best to keep my faith in the Lord that He would be watching over Michael while I was "away."

I was heartsick, crushed, and almost overwhelmed, but for Lisa's sake I had to act like I had it together. Had to keep my cool. Had to sound like I knew what I was doing, like I was in control, like I could fix all of this and make it right.

How could I ever tell her I felt like just the *opposite*?

9

Guilty Until Proven Innocent

o o o o o o o o o o o o o o o o o o o o o o o o o o o o o o o o o o o
I cry out for help, but no one hears me. I protest, but there is no justice.

—*Job 19:7*

Never in my entire life—not in my full comprehension of eternity—would I have ever expected to end up cooling my heels in some cold, impersonal bunker called a prison. Incarcerated. Locked up. Behind bars.

I had always strived to live honorably, had never been in trouble with the law before this day. I had served my country not once but *twice*, receiving awards for my service and having been honorably discharged both times. This was beyond my real of human comprehension.

It was like an out of body experience where I knew it was happening—but it was nonetheless surreal. Never in my wildest dreams had I ever thought to myself: "You better be careful, Rob, you could wind up in prison!"

Not once in all my fifty-two years had I ever pictured sitting in a jail cell, no socks, no underwear, whiling away the endless daylight hours, idly striking up conversations with total strangers, just for something to do. Chatting with hard-looking men who had been around the block a time or two, and then some.

We talked about sports scores, the terrorist attack on the World Trade Center towers in New York, and why each of us was in lock up.

Or about our ex-wives…

Yet that was exactly where I found myself one bright and sunny Texas morning after one of the longest single nights of my entire life! I knew it hadn't all been just some crazy nightmare, and that's what made it so shocking.

To feel the cold hard bunk beneath my thin mattress was to awaken to stark reality. I could hear the constant shuffle of laconic and shiftless feet as prisoners were let in and let out. The echoes of steel doors slamming and guards yelling orders up to sixteen hours a day filled the claustrophobic bunker.

The few windows that provided meager amounts of light we gratefully received were nonetheless aimed at the sky. It felt as if I was in a deep, bottomless hole and that my hope had been buried along with me.

I watched with wonder the endless array of Hispanic, Indian, Asian, black and white prisoners. For the most part they all kept to their ethnic pockets within the common area when we were permitted to come out of our little concrete burrows. The sum of that time would rarely be more than eight hours—total.

It was simply unbelievable, inconceivable, indescribable and, for now, entirely unavoidable!

Again and again I heard myself mentally repeating the same, tired mantra: "I can't believe I'm *in* here. I *can't* believe I'm in here. I can't believe I'm in *here*. I can't believe *I'm* in here."

I wanted to simply pinch myself, bring myself back to life, and discover that I was sitting on the couch in my wonderful home, dozing off in front of the television, where an all-day, all-night Court TV marathon was playing an endless loop of cheesy prison flicks starring faded action heroes in less than meaty roles.

It was the ultimate nightmare, yet I could barely sleep...

No, that's not quite right, either: It was like a *waking* nightmare, a horror movie come to life, but I was no movie star and there was no director to yell "cut!" at the end of the day. There was no hot tub or catered dinner to return to, no stunt double to shuffle back and forth from the cell to the common area for me. I was all alone. Robbed of my freedom.

Incarcerated...

My crime? Marrying—then divorcing—the wrong woman.

My sentence? Only time would tell...

The days were hard and long and tiring and worrisome and, to make matters even worse, I didn't know anyone. Not a single soul. I honestly think, out of all of it—the betrayal from Bonnie, the not knowing how long I'd be there, the bland and tasteless food, the cramped quarters, the awkward sleeping conditions, the cold—being utterly alone was the worst part of it all!

All my life, I had always been part of a bigger group, a den in cub scouts, a pack in boy scouts, a crew, a squad, a unit, a department, some part of a collective "whole" that swallowed me up and welcomed me inside.

In the Navy, even while struggling in boot camp, where trust and friendship were as hard to come by as a hot bath, I'd been surrounded by like-minded individuals who made up a larger organization of like-minded individuals.

Guys my age and weight and disposition who could always—*always*—be counted on for a quick game of cards, a firm pat on the back, or even an off-color joke when times got too tough.

Years later, after my military service had ended, I turned to the church for the same kind of fellowship—albeit without the off-color jokes and blue language! (But plenty of pats on the back to go around!)

There I found friendship, encouragement, companionship—and even my future wife and the mother of my son, Linda. It was a warm, safe, *sacred* place to go, not just for communion—but to *commune* with other similar souls who were all searching for the same exact thing.

Here, in jail, I knew none of the daily rituals, none of the boring routine. Some of the men I was sequestered with weren't exactly hard-core "lifers," but they had definitely seen the inside of a jail cell—or even two or three—before. They had "the look." And more than the look, they had "the attitude."

These hard, stone men with nicotine faces and whiskey voices knew just how to hold themselves, knew the patterns and ups and downs of a day "on the inside," knew exactly how to work the system, how to avoid getting caught, and even more importantly acted accordingly to stave off the boredom of another day inside and keep their heads straight.

I knew no such tricks…

Slowly, quietly, I started to observe others in my jail cell. What I saw wasn't as disturbing as I'd perhaps imagined "on the outside." Movie cons—and even those caricatures they flaunt on TV—are always bigger than life, monsters, giants who troll the prison yard looking for easy marks.

But while the men I quartered with weren't exactly *monsters*, some were certainly more than menacing and not exactly the type of rough and tumble individuals I would have wanted to invite over to my house for dinner. Or even know my home address or phone number!

I understood all too well their situations, however. "There but for the grace of God go I" is a helpful mantra to remember when simply trying to survive behind the institutional walls of today's modern American prison. I knew that many of those hard, tight-eyed men I bunked down with each night hadn't been *born* bad—they'd been made that way.

Lack of money, lack of one parent or the other, lack of food, lack of a roof over their head or a soft place to sleep or schooling or health insurance—it all went to make the various men I shared a cell with in my new home.

I had been fortunate enough to have been born into a good family, a close family—and they'd helped me rise above the baser temptations that called to such men. Men without the good fortune and many blessings that had filled my cup to runneth over during the course of my young life.

"There but for the grace of God go I…"

More than understanding the life these men had come to lead, however, I forgave it. After all, Jesus teaches us to "hate the sin, but love the sinner." And inside the prison walls, away from their hoodlum friends and dysfunctional families, it was easy to see the good intentions and missed opportunities that brought these men to their current states of temporary disrepair.

I prayed for them nightly, and hoped they'd do the same for me…

Yet I saw signs of life—*spiritual* life—in these men, these strangers, and more so than I would have ever imagined existing behind bars. When I saw someone pray quietly over their food before eating, I took careful note to talk to them later. Eventually, this simple practice would help pull me out of the despair that had a stranglehold on my emotions. It blessed me.

In more ways than one…

I first met a black man, a preacher who, even without his robes, looked wise beyond his years. I did not know why he was in jail. It was considered rude to ask another inmate the taboo question, "What are you in for?", although they do it on TV all the time. If they wanted to tell you, they'd tell you. Besides, it did not matter what he'd done, it only mattered what he was *doing*.

We talked about the Lord and the many ways in which God had revealed Himself to each of us in our individual lives. We prayed together for our families, loved ones, and friends. It felt good to find a kindred spirit among the riffraff, and for the first time since my incarceration I felt a sense of hope that all would not be lost. That my time inside the walls of this institution would not be entirely wasted on crossword puzzles and dumb blonde jokes!

Soon he introduced me to another black man and, before long, we all talked together about the growing nature of our spiritual selves. About the lives of men, of prisoners, of the innocent. I also noticed a Hispanic man about my age talking about the Lord to another, younger man.

This occasion filled my sore heart with pride and I talked to him later and we prayed together, too. Later I would come to introduce all of these separate, wounded men to one another and it felt good to bring the different parts of the body of Christ together as a whole.

It helped each of us to strengthen one another with our shared faith…

On the third day of my incarceration a young black man was transferred into our cell block. When he first entered our area, he noticed us praying. He came right over to our table and said: "I have been in this jail for three months looking for some Christians to fellowship with." Naturally, we welcomed him into our slowly growing fold with arms wide open!

This wayward young man with such strong potential had used to sing in the choir at his church and had since fallen away into a life of crime by running with the wrong crowd. Now he was here, with us, and ready to turn his life around—with God's help—and by making ourselves available to him, too.

It was a moving experience to share the love of God with these very different men from very different backgrounds, hometowns, and cultures. It was truly inspiring to see that, indeed, we were all of us brothers—in the eyes of the Lord. My experience in jail was living, breathing proof of the scripture, and my faith was strengthened by the experience as a whole.

Praying, reading the Bible, and engaging in other forms of active worship also helped to engage some of my fierce energies and frustrated emotions. I finally felt that if I could not be outside and free and helping my son deal with the horrible things that had been happening recently, then I could at least be called upon to bring comfort and hope to those who were suffering and in need within these drab prison walls.

I would just have to trust God that He would watch over my son…

The ramifications of my situation were still mind-boggling to me. Perhaps the fact that I knew little about the inner workings of the justice system in America at that time was indeed a blessing.

Though it felt like a curse at the time…

On the third day of my incarceration, I was told that my case would finally be going before a judge, who would then rule on whether or not to let me out of jail on a "Fugitive from Justice" warrant for the state of Texas.

Meanwhile, the local court could not simply let me out on my own recognizance, because I had been formerly arrested on an out of state warrant. If I did not agree to this measure, then I would have to wait until Oregon got good and ready to extradite me.

And who knew how long *that* could take?

Extradition could take weeks—if not *months*. After several days on the inside, a week was no longer as unimaginable to me as it had once been only days earlier. But a *month*? Or perhaps even *two* months? Now that was incomprehensible! Weeks sounded like months, thus months sounded like years.

I wanted out. Out into the real world, out in society, out on the streets of my city, out where I could try to get my son back. But to do that, I would have to look and act my best. Unfortunately, I had nothing on hand to aid in the massive clean up that was required as to my appearance, and with four days growth of beard marring my face, I was looking a bit more than wild. But at least I would be showered and could finally use what little soap I had left to clean up for my important court appearance.

When the big day arrived, I was transported out of the jail wing, boarded a van with several other prisoners, and taken into the Collin County courthouse where I was immediately put in a holding cell.

I was once again chained in ankle shackles that quickly chaffed my ankles raw. My hands were also handcuffed to the belt around my waist again. I thought what I had experienced beforehand was tight, but now I was forced to endure truly claustrophobic conditions.

The cell we were ordered to wait in was down a hall that was hardly four-feet wide. Had my hands not been fastened to securely to a belt around my waist, I could have stretched out my arms and touched either side of the wall with my elbows!

The cell itself was roughly 6-feet by 8-feet. It felt like a closet with a sink in it! To make matters worse, I had to wait there for several hours. Naturally, no distractions of any kind were made available to us. No magazines, no newspapers, no phone, no talking of any kind. All we could do was sit and ponder our uncertain fate. When my turn finally came it was completely humiliating to be taken into court like some kind of heinous criminal.

And all the while the knowledge burned inside me: I had not done the crime for which I had been charged!

I did not kidnap my son. I had been granted physical and legal custody of my son as his only living parent…

So why was this happening to me?!?

Fortunately, the judge presiding over my case was extremely understanding of my situation. He even had a copy of the divorce decree showing that *I* indeed had been granted custody of my son during the time I crossed state lines.

He was incredulous about the turn of events that had so recently transpired, but was nonetheless bound to uphold the law of the land and thus had to honor the warrant for my arrest. He cautiously advised me of the potential can of worms that issuing a "Fugitive from Justice" warrant could mean for me, but he wished me well in my plan to return to Oregon to get the matter straightened out by myself.

After the almost anticlimactic scene back in the courtroom, I was taken back to the Collin County Jail and returned to my cell while I was awaiting the process papers to finally be drawn up. If the paperwork was not completed soon, I would have to spend the entire weekend in jail.

I was told that I could be released on my own recognizance, but for the outstanding FBI warrant. If the FBI would simply drop their warrant, there would be no requirement for a set bail amount.

To her esteemed credit, Officer Linda Cartledge put in numerous calls to the FBI to get them to release their warrant, yet all was in vain. They obviously had bigger fish to fry, and so were apparently dragging their feet on the matter.

They were in no rush…

I have a theory about that, as well: I firmly believe that their feet-dragging was in no small part due to the efforts of my ex-wife's Private Investigator, Jeff Wilson of Eugene, Oregon, who was coincidentally—or perhaps even *not* so coincidentally—a former FBI agent who obviously still had ties with the Bureau.

I was later to learn that he had been instrumental in getting that very same warrant issued in the first place. It seems that the FBI can issue such warrants with little or no substance, and then simply drop them at will. Apparently, "investigation" is their strong point—not "justice!"

(Guess that's why they're not called the FBJ…)

The bail was set at $5,000.

Fortunately, I had that much money; *unfortunately* Lisa did not have access to my bank accounts to withdraw the funds. She *did* have enough on hand to get the services of a bonding company, and would have to pay $500 in cash for something known as a "surety bond," which was of course non-refundable. Lisa put up the bail money even as we were still awaiting word on the FBI warrant. We came to find out that after she had actually put up the money, the FBI had finally relented and so there would have been no need to pay the money in the first place.

The tedious machinations of out-processing were exasperating, but not as protracted as the intake process had been several fateful nights earlier. To meet the exacting and seemingly archaic paper procedures of the great state of Texas, I had to fill out papers and sign numerous documents until my hand was nearly cramped and useless. In between writing my life story on various forms, I was in and out of holding cells for nearly two hours before finally being escorted out of the jail.

When all was said and done, it was after 8 p.m. on a Texas Friday night before I was finally released from the Collin County Jail. (Talk about a big, fat TGIF!) I had been under arrest for four long days and three even *longer* nights. I knew more than ever what "UNDER" arrest truly meant.

I remember thinking that I had not felt anything quite like that experience since I left the coast of war-torn Vietnam after my second tour of duty and had arrived stateside to a land of peace and prosperity and politics—and perhaps even more importantly, *freedom*.

Yet there was little time to smell the roses and rest on my laurels. Now the next leg of the adventure would inevitably begin: I had to find out if Michael was still in Texas. The courts would not tell me. The DA would not tell me. The police would not tell me. Child Protective Services, or CPS, would certainly not tell me.

Yet somehow I had to find out!

I assumed that since my ex-wife Bonnie was certainly the mastermind behind all of this sad and sordid drama, she *must* know where my son was—and *why* he had been taken from me in the first place.

I called her home number and left an understandably urgent message. It was twenty-four excruciatingly long hours later before she called and said, "Michael is with me and he is safe" before hanging up the phone before I could even say anything to my ex-wife—*or* my son.

I called several more times before that endless night was over, but Bonnie would not pick up the phone. There was no longer any doubt about it: I would have to go to Oregon—and I did not know for how long.

Or even what would await me once I got there...

Before leaving on my miles-long odyssey to bring back little Michael, I contacted my old divorce attorney, Bob McCann, and asked him to get up to speed and represent me—if it was at all possible.

I knew that eventually I would need some kind of legal help, both on the offensive side, when I was going to have to use the strong arm of the law to force eventual issues, and to play defense, when Bonnie lobbed her inevitable legal volleys onto *my* side of the court. And so I told Bob that I was coming to Oregon immediately and would be there in three days.

Or less, if I had anything to do with it!

I drove straight to Corvallis, Oregon—nearly 2,300 *miles*—in my eight-year-old pickup truck! It took exactly three days to get there, and I went prepared to do whatever it was going to take to get my son back. And then some. I wanted to get this matter straightened out, once and for all, in a court of law that would settle the matter for good.

The lies that must have been told by Bonnie to have me thrown in jail surely would not stand up to the truth. In the harsh light of day. On the witness stand. Sworn to oath. All throughout my long, arduous travels I prayed for there to be a peaceful resolution to this ongoing and unpleasant matter. I prayed for myself, for little Michael, for my lovely new wife and two beautiful stepchildren.

Why, I even prayed for Bonnie...

As a result, I was alternately filled with an overwhelming sense of calming peace and serenity, while at the same time I was so wound up with adrenaline I could hardly keep my foot off the gas pedal! My ex-wife had stolen my son—and I had to go rescue him from this madness!

When I got to my old divorce attorney's office, Bob showed me the legal documentation that had eventually resulted in my incarceration. Apparently, Bonnie had gotten custody of Michael, by way of default, in a hearing that she had requested back in June of 2001. But I had never even gotten *notice* of that hearing. Not from Bonnie, not from the courts, not from Oregon, not from Texas!

Not from anyone...

I was incredulous. Somehow Bonnie had finagled her way through the entire Oregon court system and found herself another judge. A judge who obviously did not have any background whatsoever with our divorce proceedings, prior *or* current. She had even submitted sworn affidavits saying that she did not know where I was, nor did she know how to get in contact with me to advise me of the hearing. (This despite the fact that she had hired a private detective to track me down!)

On the basis of her sworn affidavits, the new judge had duly granted her "petition for custody" of my little Michael. Furthermore, Bonnie had claimed that on last April of 2001 that I had committed "custodial interference," which was a lie. *She* did not have custody at that time.

We did not even have *joint* custody. I had custody...

I went into court thinking that surely the judge would see what had gone on up to this point—and that all of this would surely get resolved in a matter of minutes once the truth had finally come out. I was arraigned and the judge gave me a release agreement drafted by the District Attorney, which said I was not to have contact with Bonnie or Michael "pending the dissolution case before the court."

I was being ordered not to get in touch with either Bonnie or Michael in the interim and there was *no* dissolution case pending. This was ludicrous. My choice was to take the release—or go to jail until they could set a hearing date. Yet that would likely be in two or three months.

Two or three *months!*

Naturally, I took the release. With the felony charge still pending against me, my old divorce attorney was out of his league. Bob hoped that a conference call with the District Attorney could get these charges dropped—and that rational behavior could finally be instituted.

Naturally, my ex-wife wanted *nothing* to do with that. In fact, to add insult to injury, she was actually claiming to be a "victim" under the victim's rights laws of the state of Oregon. The battle lines were being drawn and it was obvious that things were going to get very ugly.

Poor Bob McCann, to his esteemed credit, said that he could no longer represent me because he was not that well versed in criminal law, and because he felt I had grounds to bring a "just cause" lawsuit against the Benton County DA *and* the Albany, Oregon Police Department.

Bob's law partner, James Delapoer, was also the legal counsel for the Albany Police Department. It would have been a potential conflict of interest if he were to represent me. Therefore, Bob recommended me to an attorney in Corvallis, Oregon named Stephen Ensor.

I spent a total of nine days in Oregon—and not a single thing was actually resolved. It took all of those nine long days to get an arraignment, be formally booked, and get fingerprinted by the Benton County Sheriff's Office.

While going through processing, a deputy called around but no one knew anything about any outstanding warrant against me. That really didn't surprise me, however, as I was beginning to see how the justice system worked for those who knew how to manipulate it. And my ex-wife, with the help of her Corvallis, Oregon attorney, Pamela Hediger, was doing a fine job of that.

I later discovered that Ms. Hediger used to work as an assistant DA with Benton County, but now practiced mostly divorce law. I was also to learn that the Benton County DA, Scott Heiser, had little or no experience in regard to divorce law and its intricate terminology. Apparently, he had no problem giving his *own* interpretation as to what my divorce decree actually contained. I had many questions regarding the handling and decision making process of the Benton County DA, but I would have to wait many months before I could get any answers.

With little to do and frustration mounting, I reluctantly returned to my home in Plano, Texas. When all was said and done, I had been gone for thirteen days. I was beat, but not *beaten*. I wanted to get home as quickly as possible, and so I drove a faster route that would get me home in half the time if I drove long and hard. I drove 1,200 miles on day one and 900 miles on the second day!

That put me home on a Saturday evening. The timing couldn't have been better. Not only was I elated to be with my family once again, but I desperately needed to be in church and feel the presence of God and commune once again with my desperately missed "church family." I had a few weeks of peace and quiet, and then I would have to fly back to Oregon for some follow up court appearances.

Just like in the Navy, it was time to put my battle gear on. Unlike in the Navy, I was all alone on this solo mission…

10

Puzzle Pieces

o o o o o o o o o o o o o o o o o o o o o o o o o o o o o o o o o o
You have closed their minds to understanding, but do not let them triumph.

—Job 17:4

Once I was safely back at our family home in Plano, Texas, I suddenly found that I faced many challenging days worth of work assembling the necessary legal documentation which would be required for the upcoming court battles with Bonnie. Even released from prison, my ex-wife's wake left me swirling in a sea of legalese and outdated paperwork!

In between fleeting moments of gratitude for my newfound sense of freedom, I would try to busy myself with the writing, organizing, digesting, and assembling of legal information for my new attorney. It was not easy: think the IRS meets the FBI meets the DA and you'll have an idea of the mountain of paperwork I faced in response to the unwarranted charges against me.

For the first time I understood what the term "paper trail" really meant...

Yet it was hardly a time of peaceful reflection for me: I still had my other various household duties to perform as a husband to my beautiful wife Lisa—and as a stepfather to my children Shannon and Derrick. Very often I would look around the empty house while Lisa was at work and the children were at school and find myself staring at the various places where Michael used to sit, remembering fondly all that we had once shared as father and son.

Sometimes simply looking just wasn't enough...

I would often get up from what I was doing—paying bills, cooking dinner, organizing my mountain of file folders, gathering paperwork for the trial—and go into his empty room and look at the books and stuffed animals still sitting forlornly on his abandoned shelves.

I would remember tucking him in at night and hearing his little voice forever asking me to "touch his head." He liked to have me gently caress his head, neck, back, and arms to help him relax—and eventually soothe him quietly off to sleep. Sometimes I would have to caress his growing legs as well, knowing that his untimely growth spurts made his muscles hurt occasionally.

When I gently caressed his feet and legs he would often let loose with an uproarious giggle because it tickled, too. There is no sound more joyous to a father's ears than to hear his little son giggling playfully in the sweet throes of his innocent childhood. I would often smile and cry at the same time, remembering what *was*.

What had been.

What could have been.

And what might never be again…

I desperately wanted my son back. Back where he belonged. Wanted him back with his family. Wanted him back so that I could hear his laugh once more, play games with him, share one of our famous picnic lunches in the park, visit the zoo with him, caress his growing arms and legs, smell his golden blond hair, hold him close, and teach him the various things that would help him become a man.

In Michael's honor—and in the hopes that he would someday soon return to his beloved old room—I hung a frame containing all of my various Cub Scout badges, Boy Scout badges, and even my Navy ribbons and medals. They had hung on the wall in his bedroom since he was a baby. Now they hung on the wall near his heirloom twin bed along with a family portrait of Michael, Linda, and I before she got too terribly sick.

I often remembered the hopes and dreams of what we had all imagined would lie ahead of us as a family. There were so very many. Now she was dead and our only son had been stolen from my arms as well.

When Bonnie took Michael, she returned him to the Greater Albany Public school system (or GAPS) in late October 2001—a total of two weeks after she picked him up. He must have been very upset about being taken away from his father and not knowing what had happened to him, and it breaks my heart to this day to know that he endured so many days without my calm and nurturing presence—let alone even my voice.

It was obvious to me why Bonnie was orchestrating this particular series of events: She *needed* that time to get Michael under control. After all, she *had* to have control, to make him do her bidding, to make *her* look good.

She had a lot of lies to keep track of, not to mention remain buried, and the first thing she had to do was make Michael do the "right things" to support her facade. And the first place she had to start was the same place Michael would be attending for the majority of his time away from her: his school.

There was only one Individual Education Plan, or IEP, in effect for Michael at the time, and without my constant vigilance on Michael's behalf, that would essentially be ignored under Bonnie's watch. Not only would Michael *not* be allowed the accommodations agreed upon a year earlier—the use of a calculator and a computer—but he would be held back in his schoolwork as well.

I had left the original two volumes of Michael's home school papers with Bonnie's pastor, Ed Sweet. Bonnie had them in her possession, but refused to share their actual content with anyone at Michael's new school.

When Michael first got into 4th grade at North Albany Elementary School, he read a 2.5 grade level book with 100% comprehension. Thereafter, they gave him books below that grade level—even down to kindergarten. In doing so, his comprehension naturally dropped off.

His lack of interest, combined with a lack of contact with his father, had a profound impact on him. In fact, his poor performance would continue until he regained contact with me. Michael was also remediated in first and second grade level math, and held there for the remainder of the year. It seems that Bonnie purposely wanted to "dumb him down," if only in order to have more control over him.

Naturally, this was not in the best interest of anyone.

Anyone but Bonnie, that is…

How could any of this—*mess*—even remotely be considered "in the best interest of the child?" Though the legal system had been manipulated by a born "con" in this case, I had to believe that they would not allow this fraud to continue once all the puzzle pieces were finally brought to light. It was the one, burning hope that kept me going through those long, dark days proceeding the upcoming trial.

Meanwhile, Bonnie Vickers knew the terms of my release forbade me to have contact with her or with my son. She sent me three letters, one each on November 2, November 9, and November 13, 2001. The content of these letters was Bonnie's pathetic attempt to get a response that would jeopardize my freedom. While proclaiming her rights under the Oregon Victim's Rights law, she was attempting to provoke me to contact her.

Meanwhile, I was denied access to copies of progress reports and IEP documentation for Michael by the Albany Public School district. Bonnie is an employee of the Albany Public School District and, while the school district's attorney claimed "neutrality," he was certainly not forthcoming with requests I submitted almost weekly beginning the end of October 2001. My first request went via an Email to Linda Hadfield on October 30, 2001. She was the main contact I had for Michael's special needs with the school district.

Immediately the Benton County District Attorney, Scott Heiser, got involved by faxing copies of my arresting warrant charges and a copy of my release agreement to the attorney for the Greater Albany School district, Mr. Schultz. This was apparently done to insinuate that I should not be entitled to my requests, even when my requests had nothing to do with my having contact with my son. To this day I believe that there is only one way that the DA got involved on the very same day as I made my request, and that way had to be by way of Bonnie!

My lawyer, Steve, went to bat for me on more than one occasion by trying to reason with deputy District Attorney Dan Armstrong on the lack of merit involved in these erroneous charges filed by an obviously vindictive ex-wife. After hours of intense negotiations, the District Attorney finally relented, realizing that the charges against me simply wouldn't hold up in court.

We negotiated a deal wherein I would plead "no contest" to a misdemeanor charge of contempt of court. Though it galled me to have to plead to anything, let alone something as onerous as contempt of court, I went along. As a result, all references to "custodial interference" and "knowingly violated a joint custody order" would be removed from the court documents.

The District Attorney wanted assurances that I would reimburse Ms. Vickers for her expenses, which she had duly submitted. All told, those expenses totaled about $6,500. Yet she still owed *me* over $5,600 from the division of a tax-sheltered annuity, as ordered in the original divorce decree, which was recorded 14 months prior. The idea of applying that amount to what was owed seemed reasonable, and so that is what we finally agreed upon.

After that was settled, I told my attorney, Steve, that I wanted him to immediately file "contempt of court" charges against Bonnie as they related to the hearing in March of 2001 where nothing had been resolved! I also wanted him to file papers requesting a "change of custody" hearing based upon the fraud that had been committed by Ms. Vickers upon myself.

Not to mention poor Michael…

Those papers were indeed filed, and within days Ms. Vickers vetoed the District Attorney's settlement with me for a reduction in charges. She now claimed that she had "additional expenses." Furthermore, she needed time to get those bills together. As was to happen time and time again in these legal proceedings, the court gave her three weeks to get her paperwork in order and return to present them.

When she did not present the required paperwork after three weeks, she was immediately given *another* four weeks to comply. Again, she failed to provide the documentation after the second term of four weeks and was given yet another three weeks to comply. It all could have been settled by the end of November, but she made it drag out until mid-February, a total of ten full weeks later!

Meanwhile, in another one of those Catch-22's that make the American judicial system eternally frustrating, the court would not schedule a custody hearing until the criminal charges and restitution were taken care of.

In my opinion, Bonnie used both the court *and* the District Attorney in this matter to perform what basically amounted to blackmail and extortion in this case. I would not be allowed to even *talk* to Michael by telephone until we got to day one of the custody hearings, now scheduled for mid-March of 2002!

As the days turned into weeks—and then *months*—Bonnie would not relent in her war of attrition and there seemed to be no legal authority who would remedy the damage I had suffered at her hands.

This experience would be a rude awakening for me.

I would continually ask myself over the coming months: "What happened? How was she able to pull off these lies? How could she so effortlessly manipulate so many well-educated and apparently competent legal professionals, some of them at the highest level of authority?"

Step-by-step, however, the various details of her behind-the-scenes battle of manipulation she waged against me were finally revealed through the documentation I eventually received through my attorney.

This vital and fascinating information would eventually include copies of legal documentation from the Benton County District Attorney files, Albany City police files, Benton County files, and Bonnie's private investigator files.

On December 4, 2001, Bonnie priority mailed Michael's suitcase to my home. It arrived six days later. This vindictive act appears to be in direct response to her being served with contempt of court papers and request for custody hearing papers. This was also an attempt to provoke me into violating my terms of release and thereby endangering my freedom.

The items received in the mail from Ms. Vickers, inside Michael's own suitcase, no less, included those things Michael personally chose to take with him when Child Protective Services picked him up on October 9, 2001—the same day Bonnie had me arrested.

When I spoke with Pastor Ed Sweet on October 22, 2001, I asked him if I could leave some clothes and 2 volumes of home school papers for Michael with him if it was okay with Bonnie. Pastor Sweet said he contacted Bonnie and that the arrangement was fine with her. The next day I left three bags of things for Michael, including his third and fourth grade home school papers. The bags of clothing included the following:

- 1 pair of new shoes
- 1 pair of new insulated snow pants
- 1 new pair of insulated gloves
- 1 new stocking hat (with a Colorado Rockies logo that Bonnie's niece gave to him for Christmas 3 years prior)
- 1 new insulated vest
- 1 pair swim trunks
- 2 pair black sweatpants
- 1 new pair of Scooby-Do earmuffs
- 3 pairs of white socks
- 3 white T-shirts
- 2 pairs of underwear
- 1 red logo T-shirt that he picked out
- 1 California logo T-shirt that his grandmother gave him last Christmas
- 1 baby seal stuffed toy that is a favorite of his
- 1 meerkat stuffed toy Michael picked out when we went to the Dallas zoo together in June of 2001
- 6 pictures of Michael at the Dallas zoo, Natural History Museum, Texas State Fair, and with me
- A note for Michael to let him know that "I was okay, I loved him, and I hoped to talk to him sometime soon," and also containing my phone number; a message that his toys and things were safe with me; and also telling him to "be good, be happy, and I was going to pray for him every day"

Also in the suitcase were some things that Michael picked out that he specifically wanted to take with him when Child Protective Services picked him up:

- 1 Dalmatian stuffed toy dog that was given to him right after his mother died when he was 2-years-old

- 1 stuffed blue puppy dog toy that he won when he went with me to the Texas State Fair in September of 2001

- 1 stuffed shark toy that he picked out when I took him to the Oregon coast aquarium on a second grade field trip

- 8 of his favorite action figure toys

All of the above things were actively taken away from Michael—by Bonnie—and mailed to me in his very own suitcase. I could only imagine the heartbreaking scene that ensued as the last, few remaining possessions he owned on this earth were boxed up and carted away.

By his so-called "psychological parent."

I still get the chills just thinking about it…

But broken dreams were not all that I received in the mail that winter: In December the attorney for the Albany Public School district, Ed Schultz, mailed me a few notes for a meeting about Michael's school progress that took place back in November. He did not send me any of the other copies as requested, and through the end of the month did not respond to my correspondence.

On December 18, Bonnie's attorney, Pam Hediger, submitted an incomplete listing of restitution documentation. This was just three days prior to the court date, and Ms. Hediger said that she would be on vacation and unavailable until after the New Year.

How convenient…

This was nothing more than yet another piece of their plan to make sure I had no contact with my son over the Christmas holidays. The total had since ballooned from $6,400 to $15,880. Yet less than a quarter of this amount had verifiable information attached. The District Attorney asked the court for a postponement for more time to contact Ms. Hediger and get the verifiable documentation. The matter was continued until January 15, 2002.

On Christmas Eve I received in the mail from Bonnie a box containing Michael's home school curriculum books, notebooks, and monthly progress notes—all of which came from the six full months in which I had home schooled him under Texas state law. This was yet another attempt at provoking me and rubbing salt in the wound that I would not have contact with my son at Christmas. There seemed to be no end to her evil ways.

Not even on what is traditionally the "happiest night of the year!"

Before I was arraigned and booked in Benton County, I had left these things with Bonnie's pastor after receiving her permission to do so. My intent was to assist the school district in their assessment for developing an IEP for Michael.

During my numerous requests for documentation with the school district, I had asked repeatedly if they had seen any of this documentation. No one with the school district provided me any verification that they had, and so I had drawn the obvious conclusion that half a year's worth of schoolwork with Michael had been virtually ignored.

All in an effort to make me look worse…and Bonnie look better.

But how much did that spiteful act cost little Michael?

Meanwhile, I struggled to get proceedings moving toward a custody hearing. At 4 p.m. on Friday, January 10, 2002, Bonnie's attorney, Pam Hediger, faxed a detailed invoice for her office's attorney fees beginning with March 20, 2001 through January 9, 2002. The rest of the requested documentation was not submitted to the District Attorney's office—*or* to my attorney's office. At my court appearance on January 15, 2002—I was still authorized by the court to appear by telephone—the matter was continued once again to two weeks later. The District Attorney did not want to take a sentencing deal, or plea, until we had full agreement on the amount of restitution.

On January 20, I received a near complete response to my repeated inquiries from Albany School District principal Ric Blasquez. I still did not have confirmation that anyone on the IEP team had actually *reviewed* the home school related documentation that I left to assist in the development of Michael's IEP. The lingering question remained as to why the school district took ten weeks to give an adequate response to my request back in October.

Why would they withhold information that was clearly within my rights as a parent to obtain?

At the January 28 court date, the felony charge was officially dropped. Finally, I was able to breathe a small sigh of relief! Still, we were far from opening the champagne. On the paperwork, the District Attorney stated: "no contact with son, Michael Carey, unless approved by court in pending dissolution case."

Yet the divorce had been granted and recorded nearly 18 months prior to this date! The fact that I had full custody out of that divorce seemed irrelevant to the Oregon judicial system. It is clear to me that Bonnie got custody—by default—only *after* a number of fraudulent actions on her part. What was still pending was a change of custody hearing, where I was asking that custody be given back to me based upon the fraud that had been committed by Ms. Vickers.

At the restitution hearing on January 12, the judge dropped the amount of restitution requested by Bonnie from a figure of close to $15,000 down to $9,800. Bonnie deliberately delayed these procedures in order to manipulate the system and deny my son access to his father and his family.

After all, she knew full well that a custody hearing could not take place until the matters of pleadings and restitution were addressed. It is obvious to me that she made this dual process last as long as she could. Meanwhile, my son was held hostage by what amounted to little more than extortion.

I was getting over some hurdles, but the race was far from over. However, following the restitution hearing I was finally able to get the Collin County Court to drop the Fugitive from Justice warrant, so there was another small sigh of relief.

Movement toward the change of custody hearing continued to drag on and on and on. At the end of February, my attorney formally requested that Bonnie produce copies of *all* medical and psychological records for Michael—from the time she took physical custody in October of 2001 through the current date. Within days of this request Bonnie would take yet another step in her continual facade of lies and misinformation. On March 1, 2001 she took Michael to Oregon Health Science University in Portland, Oregon under the guise of getting a "current medical diagnosis for autism." Yet the reported interview background information, as reflected in the content of this report, revealed how Bonnie Vickers would turn it into something much more than a diagnostic tool.

It was little more than a blatant attempt on her part to lend credibility to her ongoing fraud.

According to the report, Bonnie indicated that my son was "abducted from her custody," which is a blatant lie. She provided numerous other false details that predate her involvement in Michael's life. Amazingly, three of the doctors noted in their reports the verbatim recounting of her claim that "she had joint custody, primary responsibility for Michael after the divorce, and that Mr. Carey had abducted Michael from her care."

Bonnie made no attempt to inform me of this report until *after* it was issued, so that there would be no opportunity for me to give any input. Bonnie then made this document a part of Michael's permanent educational file. Its very presence would make it appear to have credibility, by way of the impressive credentials of the disciplinarian doctors.

Who could think of a plot so devious, so genius, so brilliant?

More importantly, how can one do battle against such a formidable foe?

The audacity of Bonnie Vickers obviously knows no boundaries. She clearly operates on the premise that her desired end justifies any and all means. Unfortunately, the gravity of this serious matter was compounded by the fact that Michael was present at these background information interviews, so once again he was subjected to hearing a lot of lies and misinformation about his very own father. He was in no position to be able to do anything but tolerate her words, and as a result Bonnie was once again able to insinuate herself into his life just that much further.

Meanwhile, Bonnie's attorney stalled on my attorney's request for disclosure copies of any medical and psychological papers concerning Michael—until just two days before the impending court date. Then Ms. Hediger stated in a letter that it was too much of a burden on Bonnie to provide a response to the request. When the judge heard this at the change of custody hearing, which began on March 18, 2002, she was incredulous.

Incredulous? Maybe.

But still there was no admonishment from the bench. Once again, Bonnie had gotten away with it…

As the March 18, 2002 hearing began, Bonnie's Private Investigator, Jeff Wilson, a former FBI agent with 28 years in law enforcement, testified in Benton County circuit court to the validity of all Emails received from Bonnie Vickers and Kimberly Dunn. Those Emails were submitted as exhibits—without objection by Bonnie's attorney, Pam Hediger—before the Benton County circuit court, Judge Holcomb presiding.

This hearing would be continued and continued, ad nauseum, over the next *three* months! Bonnie would try every lie and manipulation possible to keep me from having contact with my son. On this first hearing date, she would begin by using the testimony of her counselor, Ms. Lake of Albany, Oregon.

Ms. Lake was introduced as Michael's "counselor," yet neither my lawyer nor I had ever heard of her before, nor had we ever been given any documentation copies for Michael's "alleged" treatment—as we had requested. During a short recess, we perused each page of Ms. Lake's file on Michael. The paperwork revealed that it was mostly about Bonnie, and that Ms. Lake had been given Bonnie's typewritten, distorted version of events.

Apparently, Ms. Lake only knew *her* "truth," and Ms. Lake had never made any attempt to contact me for any possible input I might have had. Coincidentally, Bonnie began seeing Ms. Lake right after she found out that the DA had cut a deal with me in November of 2001. Ms. Lake began counseling Bonnie for "stress," following Bonnie's referral through her school district employee assistance program.

It is reasonable to expect that Bonnie *would* have a great deal of stress. After all, she had put a tremendous amount of effort into spinning her lies, and that would naturally have a devastating affect on any person who had any measure of conscience; and especially so for someone like Bonnie, who claimed she was a Christian.

As part of Bonnie's treatment plan, Ms. Lake was introduced to Michael. Ms. Lake saw Michael three times between November of 2001 and March 18, 2002. For Bonnie to present Ms. Lake as Michael's "counselor" for the "trauma" he had endured at being separated from Bonnie was nothing short of ludicrous.

The judge commented, accordingly, that if Michael was in so much need of counseling, then he should have been seen a lot more than three times in five months! In any event, the judge said that I would get some visitation rights with my son restored. More importantly, Michael could now talk to his father—after being denied that right for almost six long, lonely months! Six unnecessary months, gone forever. Six months wasted on petty court disputes and missing documents and a systematic pattern of delaying the court date as long as possible so that I could not have any contact whatsoever with my son.

Six months, gone forever.

Six months, never to be seen again.

Six months Michael and I will never, *ever* get back…

Six months. It may sound like just a short time to an adult. It is a short-term temporary duty stint to a man in the military, or an average semester to a busy student attending college. But this was a little boy we were dealing with, and to him six months might seem like two long, endless years in his innocent little eyes.

If anyone was a victim in all of this mess, it is young Michael Carey. His only living biological parent and primary care provider for the first 9 and 1/2 years of his life was ripped out of his life by way of fraud and malicious actions on the part of Bonnie Joann Vickers.

And yet this is the woman with whom Michael still lives on a day-to-day basis…

Michael had lost his mother to cancer, and his father had been ripped out of his life by a woman so selfish, so cruel, so petty, so devious that she would tell any lie—to *anyone*—as long as it allowed her to win.

She would justify any and all means toward her ultimate end.

And the end she sought was money. In order to achieve that end she would stop at nothing short of full custody of *my* son…if only in order to obtain the child support she would be awarded as a result!

At the next change of custody hearing on April 12, 2002, Bonnie Vickers stated that the purpose of her and Kimberly Dunn's trip to Dallas and Plano, Texas on May 20, 2001, was to take pictures of Michael and I to the authorities located there. However, the private investigator's report and Bonnie's testimony were inconsistent. The PI said that he had sent that information to his contact in Dallas in April 2001 for distribution to *all* local police authorities.

So why did they *really* come to Texas?

The change of custody hearing was continued to May 15, and then onto June 19 and 21. At the May hearing, the judge would only give us three hours of her time. That meant that I was flying from Texas to Oregon for a three-hour hearing that was supposed to be the conclusion of an ongoing saga that had now stretched beyond seven months!

No way!

I asked my attorney to request more time, as I could see that Bonnie was intent on making this ongoing ordeal last as long as she possibly could. The judge not only refused my request, but her actions at the next session were incomprehensible: Less than one hour into the proceedings, Judge Holcomb called a short recess, left the courtroom, and when she was gone thirty minutes my attorney asked the clerk where the judge was.

The clerk said that Judge Holcomb had "double scheduled" her time and was in another courtroom arbitrating another case. This was ridiculous! The judge came back an hour later only to tell us we had forty-five minutes, and then she was going to continue the matter over to a later court date—well into June.

I was disgusted, but had to bite my tongue and keep my eye on the prize: custody of little Michael.

When I flew to Oregon on June 18, 2002, I immediately went to the Albany Police Department, or APD. I had by now amassed a chronology of events and supporting documentation that included copies from the Albany Police files and the Benton County DA's office. Since Bonnie had submitted her police report of complaint with the APD, I decided to file my own police report regarding the *false* police report that Bonnie had filed with the Albany Police back in April 2001.

The clerk on duty told me to take a seat and wait for someone to come out and speak to me. It was nearly ninety minutes before a sergeant finally took me into a room to speak with me about my formal complaint. He asked me what I wanted done with this complaint. I asked him to look at the documentation and see for himself the fraud that had been committed.

He would take my report, but would not read it *or* look at the documentation attached to the summary. He said, "the Benton County District Attorney has closed this file and they would not open it unless the District Attorney directed them to open it."

I advised my attorney of these events, and he was not surprised. He said, "Facts are less important than they might seem. The District Attorney normally chooses which side of an issue he will come down on, and he is not likely to change his mind thereafter."

I nonetheless instructed my attorney to at least try to have the District Attorney look at these documents, which clearly show that Bonnie had not only lied to him, but had used him as a pawn in her ongoing struggle for complete domination of both Michael and myself!

Talk about an eye opening experience! Here I had direct evidence of fraud, and the police that I thought were sworn to uphold the law and protect the citizenry was telling me that justice is selective and arbitrary, even politically correct, as to what they choose to do.

I suddenly realized that I had a false sense of expectation that a call to 9-1-1 would give me an appropriate response of help when I was genuinely in need of assistance. I had presented the legal authority with documentation showing that they were clearly lied to, and they did not want to hear it because they had already decided to believe Bonnie's lies fourteen months earlier. It was a classic case of "don't confuse me with the **facts**, because I have already made up my mind."

At the hearing on June 19, Kimberly Dunn was asked if she knew where "Michael and Robert had gone after they left Albany on April 2, 2001." She said that she did not have any idea. Yet the Emails that Kimberly wrote to her Private Investigator, Jeff Wilson, indicated that she *did* know.

As a result, she was shown several Emails that Mr. Wilson previously stated were, in fact, Emails sent to him *by* Kimberly Dunn. She was specifically asked about an Email she wrote to Private Investigator Wilson on April 11, 2001. In that electronic correspondence, she quoted Bonnie Vickers as writing: "the downside is that R has legal custody, therefore it was not technically custodial interference."

Kimberly was asked if she had discussed this situation with Bonnie Vickers, to which she responded that she "did not recall." Kimberly Dunn was also asked when she and Bonnie picked Michael up after I was arrested on the charge of kidnapping—which was subsequently reduced to "custodial interference." She said that they picked Michael up at about noon on October 10, 2001.

Yet the ticket stub provided for restitution shows that they did not arrive in Dallas until nearly eleven p.m. on the tenth of October. Therefore, there is no way that they could have picked Michael up until the next morning, October 11. Meanwhile, due to their callous carelessness, my son was in CPS custody in a strange environment, away from his father, and not knowing what would happen for nearly two entire days.

48 hours might not seem long to you or I, but to little Michael it must have felt like *forever*...

On the final day of testimony, June 21, 2002, Bonnie was asked if she realized that "Mr. Carey had legal and physical custody of Michael at the time she filed a police report stating that Mr. Carey had committed custodial interference." Bonnie replied that she did not know the procedures or legal terms involved in such a matter.

She added that she was just following the lead of the authorities in the legal system. When asked what she told the District Attorney, she said that she "did not recall" and "did not understand the procedures." When asked if she had legal counsel before going to the police with her claim of custodial interference, she responded that she "could not remember."

When confronted with a copy of her attorney's itemized billings showing that she clearly *had* talked to her attorney on several occasions *before* going to the police, only then did her attorney concede that Ms. Vickers was "under legal counsel at the time she went to the District Attorney and the police."

When asked if she told the grand jury that she had joint custody, Bonnie replied that "she did not remember." She *did* remember, however, that she was the only person to testify to the grand jury. When asked why she didn't tell someone that the indictment was incorrect in stating that Mr. Carey had committed custodial interference, she said that she "did not understand what the procedure was." When asked if she was happy when the grand jury came down with an indictment that would lead to the felony arrest of Mr. Carey, she finally had to admit that she was.

In regard to the affidavit Bonnie Vickers signed on May 09, 2001, in which she claimed to have used "due diligence" in trying to "contact Mr. Carey," she was asked why she did not utilize the addresses that she and Kimberly Dunn had given to Private Investigator Wilson. Again, Bonnie had no answer.

When asked why she chose to advertise in the Corvallis and Boise, Idaho newspapers, when all the while Emails showed that she suspected that Mr. Carey was in Dallas, Texas and was in contact with his father and Lisa Jergins, Bonnie claimed that she was "not certain that Mr. Carey was not in Boise." When asked why she did not advertise in the newspaper where Mr. Carey's father resides—Shelton, Washington—or in the newspaper where Lisa Jergins lives—Plano, Texas—she again had no answer. When asked if she checked to see if there was a newspaper in either place, she said "No."

Bonnie was asked if she knew that "the felony charge against Mr. Carey had been dropped." She said she did not remember. When asked if she had received restitution for her expenses, which she had claimed in her "complaint against Mr. Carey," she said that she had more expenses than what had been paid. She further claimed to have "additional travel and legal expenses that have not been paid for." The court was then advised that there had already been a restitution hearing and that Bonnie Vickers had been given full restitution for all reasonable expenses that she had submitted.

Time and again Bonnie raised lie after lie, yet the judge seemed compelled to let her run out her allegations, perhaps to avoid any potential of an untimely appeal? She had expertly used this same strategy in the divorce proceedings more than two years prior.

It is apparent that Bonnie...never...quits.

Never...

This woman who was a teacher of children, under legal counsel, had two bachelor's degrees in education and had performed some graduate studies work did not "know the procedures or legal terms involved in such a matter." My attorney's comment on her testimony is that she was disingenuous in her responses.

That is legalese for lying under oath...

Finally, the judge said that she had heard enough and would take all the information presented "under advisement." She was going on vacation for two weeks and would render a decision at a later date. How frustratingly nebulous this was for those of us whose lives were hanging in the balance. In the meantime, I simply wanted more time with my son and I requested that the judge give me at least that much while I twiddled my thumbs waiting for her ruling...

11

Pain is Inevitable, But Misery is Optional

o o o o o o o o o o o o o o o o o o o o o o o o o o o o o o o o o o

We found out firsthand in our case that the government institutions really do believe that our children belong to them. We have to be able to protect our families.

—**Robert Calabretta,** *Father of the California family whose suit against Children's Services resulted in a landmark 9th Circuit decision*

Thus far, I have had nothing even remotely *close* to the Benton County visitation guidelines for non-custodial parents. Even as late as mid-July 2002 I was *still* waiting for the judge to give me some form of that ever-elusive justice I had been searching for since this whole mess began back in October of 2001.

Bonnie has done her best to make sure that I had the least amount of contact with my son as possible. She has literally held him captive, not unlike a terrorist holds a prisoner while telling him lies in an active campaign of brainwashing.

On June 24, 2002 I made what I thought was a reasonable request for an overnight visit to take Michael to see his grandparents. He had not seen either of them for at least eighteen months, and I thought it was just about time for them all to see each other. Bonnie had had Michael in her control for nine long months, and had not made one single attempt to take him to visit them. They had even tried to contact their grandson by telephone, and she refused to return their calls—or even *take* their calls.

Even if they had known that Bonnie would allow them to see Michael, they could not travel the distance to Oregon due to ongoing health issues. I made a request to take my son on an overnight visit to see both sets of grandparents.

Bonnie denied that request, and I had to take the matter to the court in a telephone conference on July 17, 2002.

The judge allowed that visit, but at the same hearing the judge ruled that it was still in "the best interest of Michael to remain in Ms. Vickers' custody" because "in the last nine months he has now made friends in school and has a reported attachment to Bonnie's dog."

Her *dog*?!?

I was flabbergasted.

I asked the judge: "Does this mean that you are going to ignore Ms. Vickers' obvious fraud?"

The judge responded: "This court is not prepared to rule on whether her actions were fraudulent or not. This court is only ruling on what changes have taken place since Ms. Vickers gained custody of Michael and the court's opinion is that there are not enough significant changes to warrant a change of custody."

I went into this change of custody hearing asking for custody based upon the fact that Bonnie had committed fraud. That was the foundation of my argument and now the judge said she was "not prepared to rule on the fraud." I could make no sense of this ruling. None whatsoever. Bonnie had only received custody of my son by fraud and had manipulated the system to delay proceedings as long as possible. This gave her time—time to put Michael in a situation of survival. That survival meant making the best of things: making friends, living a normal life, forming attachments to family pets, trying to be happy while he waited, desperately waited, to be reunited with his father.

But more than anything else, however, Bonnie's lies got her *possession*. I am told that possession is 9/10ths of the law, even if it *is* possession by way of fraud. My attorney advised me that there was no way that I could hope for an appeal to overturn this decision.

Instead, the court directed me to submit a "proposed transitional visitation" and to try to "work things out" between Bonnie and myself. I told the court that based upon previous actions, I doubted that we could do that. I requested that a court date be set to deal with visitation in the near future. The judge agreed and scheduled a date—September 6, 2002—to hear both sides on the issue of visitation.

I asked my attorney, Steve Ensor, to take my chronology of events summary and supporting documentation to the District Attorney. He did so, and the Assistant District Attorney, Dan Armstrong, refused to even look at the documentation. My attorney told him that the facts shown in Bonnie's Emails to her Private Investigator alone indicate that she committed fraud.

The Assistant District Attorney responded by saying that he "…did not care to hear anything regarding the names Vickers or Carey." He did not want to "ever hear anything about them again."

It was obvious to me that the District Attorney's office did not want to admit to their errors, nor how they had been used in the conspiracy manipulated by one Bonnie Vickers. No wonder they never wanted to hear her name uttered in their hallowed halls again!

I might have sued the District Attorney for "just cause" as my original attorney, Bob McCann, had advised me back in November of 2001, but I could not find an attorney anywhere with a license to practice in Oregon who would even take on the case. The overwhelming reason for this as stated by each one I contacted was that the immunity laws in the state of Oregon make it nearly impossible to succeed.

There *are* attorneys that specialize in police misconduct, but that is different than going after a fellow attorney. They do not want to go after one of their fellow Oregon State Bar members. It is like trying to get one doctor to testify against another in a malpractice suit. They just will not do it.

Local trial-law attorneys reportedly dislike the attitude and unprofessional manner of the Benton County District Attorney, Scott Heiser, but they also realize it would be the kiss of death to their practice if they were even remotely involved in litigation that shed a negative light on the District Attorney's actions: Every case they took from that point on would be jeopardized. They would not be able to get an audience for a plea bargain, and any client they might manage to get would be the brunt of paybacks from the District Attorney's office on *their* attorney.

As the court directed, I submitted my proposal for visitation that would include a transition phase. I sent that to my attorney on July 25, 2002 and waited for Bonnie's counter offer.

And waited.

And waited.

And waited…

In the end, I would wait until three days before the court date in *September* before I would even see a partial response from my ex-wife.

In the meantime, making arrangements for visitation with Michael as the court directed resulted in the same routine. On July 25, 2002 I asked Bonnie to check her calendar for an acceptable weekend where I could see Michael before school started up again in the fall. She told me that she would tell me on July 29 when I called to talk to Michael. At the conclusion of my talk with Michael, I told him that I was trying to work out arrangements with Bonnie to come see him in August so that we could go see his grandparents again in Washington.

Naturally, *he* didn't have any problem with that idea.

Then I talked to Bonnie and she told me that Michael was "not ready" for another trip to Washington because it was "too hard on him." I did not want to get into it with her, and tried another tactic. I asked again for a weekend that was open, and suggested that we could "work out the details" later when my attorney got back from vacation.

I asked what weekend was open.

She said, "None."

I asked, "Are you telling me that I cannot have visitation with my son in August?"

She said, "No, I am not saying that. I wish you would come up with a plan for visitation here in Albany."

I asked her once again, "What weekend can I have visitation with Michael?" Finally, she told me "August 24th." I told her that I would make plans to be in Oregon on August 23rd and pick up Michael in the morning on August 24th.

At this point, she steered the conversation back to "how hard this is on Michael."

I told her that I did not agree with her estimation at all. I said, "He had a good time the last visit and there were absolutely no signs of any distress on his part." I added, "If it is so hard on Michael for me to take him to Washington as you claim, then how come it would not be difficult if *you* took him to Washington?"

She replied, "Things are different now."

I responded by saying, "I know they are different, because now you have custody. If I had told you what activities you could do and where you could have visitation with Michael when I had custody of him, then I would never hear the end of it."

At that point in the "conversation" she hung up on me and apparently left the phone off the hook.

Unfortunately, that is where the conversation ended.

It should be obvious by now that Bonnie is obsessed with control over *having* all the information—and *giving out* very little. She made every effort to micro manage my visitation time with Michael. She wanted a comprehensive itinerary of times, places, and activities. She insisted that Michael call her twice a day. Even in the beginning stages of reconnecting with my own son, I was forced to comply with her demands—or be faced with not seeing my son at all. What I objected to was how she manipulated him emotionally on the telephone.

The first time he talked to her during one of my visitations, she had him in tears.

With intervention from my attorney, I eventually *did* get the visitation I requested. Michael and I had a great time. At the end of the visit, when I turned him back over to his legal "captor," Michael gave me a hug, turned his head up, and gave me a kiss. That was the way he used to be with me, before Bonnie got him in her clutches.

It broke my heart to have to give my own son back to his ex-stepmother. Can you imagine? The concept is purely ridiculous, and yet it is my day-to-day reality. The whims and caprices of this emotionally unstable woman rule the life of my only son. Every phone call, every visit, every letter, every card, every gift—is overshadowed by her larger-than-life persona and demanding tactics.

When will this madness end?

And what did I ever do to deserve it?

Two days before the September 6, 2002 court date, Bonnie's visitation counter proposal looked more like a work release and parole order than a visitation decree! I continually have to realize that Michael and I are, quite literally, *prisoners* of this unstable woman. This partial proposal of hers was yet another stall tactic, and the blatant transparency of her legal maneuvering was enough to make me—and my lawyer—nauseous.

Immediately after sending this proposal over by fax to my attorney, Bonnie's attorney suggested that we reschedule the court hearing so more time could be given to "negotiate." Instead, I instructed my attorney to press for the court date, and on we went.

In court on September 6, 2002, I appeared by telephone. Before getting into more details of Bonnie's proposal, she had to lay out more of her unfounded accusations. Those accusations were bizarre at best, with no supporting evidence *or* testimony.

They were obviously intended to create fear and caution, but by this time I thought surely "this judge has heard and seen enough." Yet, amazingly, the judge seemed intent on letting Bonnie vent her myriad frustrations and endless accusations.

More time was wasted on her insipid banality, and when she was done with that the rest of her visitation counter proposal was finally revealed. She expected that the transition to full "long distance visitation" would take two years. She expected that three out of four visitation periods would take place in Albany—including three out of four weeks in the summer.

To add insult to injury, Bonnie demanded that when Michael finally *would* be allowed to come to Texas, that I would pay all of her expenses as well as his! Naturally, this would include her airfare and lodging, if and when she chose to stay in Texas during Michael's visit.

In my turn to speak, I told the judge that "three years after I first petitioned the court for relief, I am back in court seeking relief once again. It will never end until you, Judge Holcomb, lay it out comprehensively and refuse to give her wiggle room."

I then went over my proposal and it was deemed reasonable. Future visitation would be based on Benton County standard long distance guidelines, with the exception of the first time flight of Michael to his home in Texas. I would have to fly to Portland to meet him at the gate, and at the end of his visit I would fly with him back to Portland to turn him over to Bonnie.

If she insisted that Michael was not ready to fly as an unaccompanied minor the next time he was scheduled for a visit, then *she* would have to pay for her own airfare to fly with him to and from Texas. I discussed the fact that I don't get regular reports from her on the big things Michael has done, let alone a daily schedule of his events, yet when I have visitation she expects details, details, details. This is ridiculous! Her micro-management ends up interfering with my visitation time with Michael.

Three months after the September hearing, there would still be no order prepared by her attorney. Since she got her fraudulently based order for change of custody "by default" signed on July 23, 2001—17 months prior—I have nothing in writing that gives me any rights whatsoever to even have visitation with my son.

So much for happy endings…

Epilogue:
What Price Justice?

o o o o o o o o o o o o o o o o o o o o o o o o o o o o o o o o o o o

*Teenagers in foster care often call the abuse line, hoping an investi-
gation will allow them to return to their parents, which almost all
children prefer to foster care. Children know that even the worst parents love them.*

—Foster Parent Trainer

I found out the hard way that the American justice system is not a defender of the *victim*, but instead a defender of the one who best utilizes "the system," whether it be by pretense, politics, or outright manipulation.

Our justice system is only as good as those who administer it, through the power we give them when we take advantage of our right to vote. I also found out that when a person brings a false charge against another, they are virtually *immune*, as worded so poignantly in the following White House address from the President of the *National Congress for Fathers and Children*:

> *There should be an attachment of penalties to the act of falsely creating allegations,
> charges or the dissemination of information...The **National Congress for
> Fathers and Children** would hope that the legislation eventually would be
> enacted so as to make the penalty for fabricating allegations...and perpetuating the
> dissemination of such information to be equal to the penalty associated with the
> offense which is being accused.*
>
> *I recently have reviewed many cases where individuals were accused of crimes
> that have as much as a possible life sentence with a mandatory prison sentence. A
> person who falsely raises this accusation is typically facing only a misdemeanor
> based upon the filing of a false police report or other similar misdemeanor statute
> with a virtual guarantee of probation.*
>
> *In the assessment of the possible benefit to the accuser and the prejudice which
> attaches to the accused, which is frequently impossible to reverse, this may be seen
> as an acceptable risk by many, knowing that the allegation in and of itself will typ-*

ically have the desired result: causing significant prejudice, causing limitation of contact and access between the accused individual and the child.

*All of this has the effect of not only destroying the children's innocence and naiveté, but also of allowing significant time for the relationship between that accused individual (typically the **parent**) and the minor child to be destroyed. The doubt and psychological damage to the children's ability to form the relationship, the polarization created by the charges in and of themselves, typically requires long term psychiatric intervention and in many ways are **fait accompli** after the mandatory reporting and involvement of the funded state agencies.*

*Knowingly falsifying information or disseminating information so as to require the mandatory reporting or investigation or prosecution of a parent as a means to justify the interruption of the parent/child relationship should carry a monetary penalty and threat of incarceration which is equal to the crime falsely charged. Bearing false witness was considered such a major offense as to deserve its own Commandment [**See Ten Commandments: Exodus 20 at 20:16**], yet this problem is not even addressed in divorce and custody proceedings...*

[**Source**: Excerpted from a statement by **Travis Ballard**, President of the *National Congress for Fathers and Children* at The White House for a Meeting on "Supporting the Role of Fathers in Families" on November 27, 1995.]

My concerns extend far beyond the larger question of "justice for all." Instead, I am continually concerned for the welfare of my own child while in Bonnie Vickers' care. Without contact with anyone other than those family members or friends of whom *she* approves, my son has no recourse to outside influences outside of her small, bitter, twisted world.

Young Michael has been intimidated, browbeaten, and all but brainwashed—and all at her mercy alone. My heart breaks for the things she has told him about me, about my new wife, Lisa, and about what we stand for as people, as parents, as a family. The emotional baggage she has created inside his fragile little mind is enough to fill countless psychological warehouses, and still the subterfuge continues.

Throughout our short time together, all Michael ever had as a constant in his life was his father. Through his mother's sickness, I was there. Through his infancy, I was there. Through his schooling, I was there. For dinners, for backrubs, picnic lunches, movies, TV, Disney songs—I was there.

And yet now the positive influence I had on my son has all but vanished. With each passing day the bond frays a bit, the tie that binds us loosens, and Bonnie gains a foothold in Michael's life. The damage she has already done is unforgivable. The damage she might yet do is truly horrifying.

She has lied to so many people.

Including my son…

More than emotional damage, I am further concerned about the physical harm she might do to young Michael. And not without good reason: I am convinced that she has some serious psychological issues that are kept under a tight lid, and which could "pop" at any moment.

Are my feelings ungrounded? Hardly: I know she is the fourth sibling out of a total of six. Meanwhile, both siblings number *three* and number *five* have been diagnosed with mental issues including paranoid schizophrenia. They take medication to keep their "lids" on.

Bonnie has stated to me that she has suffered emotionally from long-term abuse at the hands of a stepfather and always had a very poor, mostly estranged, relationship with her biological father until his death.

No wonder she has issues with *me*.

As a man, but more importantly, as a *father*…

Furthermore, it is my opinion that her unresolved feelings from childhood and additional paranoia led to her training in the martial arts, not to mention an accumulation of many weapons, which are still in her possession.

She has two handguns a .38 and a .357, two rifles, an over/under shotgun .22, and a .306-hunting rifle. She also has a machete, Chinese throwing stars, martial arts throwing knives, and a large hunting knife that she used to keep under her pillow at night, and presumably still does. How can my son be safe in such a house of horrors?

What if scared little Michael enters her room in the middle of the night and is mistaken for an intruder?

What if he stumbles on the cache of weapons one day, unsupervised?

What if he mistakes one of her weapons for a *toy*?

The questions—and dangers—are endless…

Bonnie is well-trained in the martial arts and, in fact, is currently one test beneath having her black-belt in karate. At our wedding on October 27, 1994, her former pastor was quoted as saying, "She hates to lose and will do whatever it takes to win."

That should have served as my final warning…

Now my son and I are living in the shadow of those very words, for she has indeed won. And yet at what cost? The legal authority may have spoken, but justice has definitely *not* been served. The legal authorities want to believe that someone like Bonnie Vickers, who holds a position of respect and authority in the community as a public school teacher, is indeed trust*worthy*.

In 9 out of 10 cases, perhaps, they would be right in their assumption. After all, most people would not have the audacity to present fraudulent claims to the authorities, lie in affidavits, and commit perjury.

Unfortunately, Bonnie Vickers is not like *most* people. To her winning is everything, at any cost, no matter who gets hurt or who she has to lie to along the way.

The laws of the great state of Oregon do not want to hinder people from bringing their complaints to the authorities, and the authorities are bound by law to receive and trust that citizens who come forth with claims are being forthright. Initially, I believe that the legal authorities were doing what they thought was right, but now that the facts are out in the open, it is time for the legal authorities to correct the wrong done by way of Ms. Vickers' fraud.

If she is allowed to get away with her actions, then she will only believe that it is permissible to repeat this kind of behavior on another occasion. Perhaps what is even worse for society, however, is the fact that if *others* know that this sort of behavior is tolerated, then this becomes a legal *precedent*.

Yet I, for one, did not serve my country in the military in two separate conflicts—twice in Vietnam and again in preparation for Desert Storm—to uphold the laws of the Constitution of the United States, only to see this sort of action pressed upon the life of my child, myself, or any other citizen of these hallowed United States.

If this sort of mindset is allowed to prevail in Oregon, and a handful of other states for that matter, then how long will it be before the other states adopt *similar* laws? I do not believe that the majority of citizens realize that their status as parents is in such a precarious situation.

If they did, there would be riots in the streets!

Instead, people like myself find out too late what the consequences are, simply for allowing their child to have contact with someone who can bring suit for visitation or custody rights as a psychological fixture in the life of their child.

I have heard of other cases where non-blood related people obtained the rights to a child. The most famous landmark case was the "Sleeper" case in Salem, Oregon, where a non-biological male step parent was awarded legal custody. In this particular case, the father was disabled and could not work. Instead, the mother worked full time to support the family. After the divorce, the mother intended to move with her daughter back to her home on the island of Guam. The court ruled that this was not in the best interest of the child, and awarded custody to the non-biological male.

The second case unfolded when a couple in Portland, Oregon hired a woman in Russia to serve as their housekeeper. She brought her 3-year-old daughter with her. At the end of four years of service, the woman wanted to move back to Russia with her child. Instead, the couple went to the court and got visitation rights because they said they had "established a relationship with the child." Amazingly, the court took the woman's passport and ordered her not to leave the state of Oregon!

The third case involves a biological mother and a non-biological male. The couple were getting a divorce and another woman cared for the child while the mother worked. As happens so often, there was a lot of hostility in the dissolution of the marriage. As a result, the woman who was little more than the child's caretaker went to court and got legal custody of the couple's child!

Where are the *biological* parents' rights?

Just a few years ago several Native Americans took white adoptive parents, and others, to court because the Native American children were being denied access to their cultural roots—and they were prevailing in the courts. Meanwhile, people with legitimate adoptive parental rights were *losing*.

Why are natural parents being stripped of their rights when there is no evidence of neglect, abuse, or child endangerment? Are we living in the land of the free and the home of the brave? Or are we simply living under the shadow of a Communist mindset where the state owns and directs the future of the child?

The state seems to be tearing up the institution of the American family, even when it is well documented that doing so has all but destroyed the fabric of our modern, "latchkey" society. We have the God-given right to bear children, yet now the state presumes the right to *steal* that child and tell the parent that they really only have **one** main responsibility—to pay child support!

But isn't it the children who are really ***paying***?

I have come to believe the saying, "pain is inevitable, but misery is optional," so I choose to utilize the access I have to my son...to let him know that I love him, pray for him, and encourage him. In time I hope he will grow strong and be able to make choices for himself. In the meantime, I must remain vigilant for his sake and pick my battles. Daily I have to choose to let God have the outrage I feel, let God have the pain I can hardly bear. I must let my fellow citizens know of this danger in the hope that they will not befall this same fate. We must protect our rights and especially the rights of our children.

APPENDIX A

The Chronology

The following appendix is a summary of the chronology of events throughout the legal proceedings documented in this book. In fact, it is the very same summary I asked the Albany Police Department and the Benton County District Attorney to review. Yet representatives of *both* agencies refused to even look at the summary, or the accompanying documentation (See *Appendix B*).

Many of the documentation pages are from the files of these two agencies, and were provided to me in preparation for my defense when felony charges were pending against me. In *Appendix B* I have included the most pertinent documents, but certainly nowhere near *all* of the documentation I accumulated during this ordeal.

It is my hope that they will help you to better understand the facts of this case...

CHRONOLOGY OF EVENTS:

By Robert D. Carey

The following is a summary of the events that occurred between March of 2001 and June of 2002. The documentation attached (See *Appendix B*) includes copies provided by and from the Benton County DA's files, copies of Bonnie Vickers' Private Investigator, Jeff Wilson's, files, copies of documents recorded in Benton County, and copies of documentation that were entered as exhibits into Benton County circuit court, Judge Janet Holcomb presiding:

March 2001

The divorce decree directed Ms. Vickers to return specific items to me, such as document copies, copies of computer diskettes, and the copy of my computer hard drive. Since the judge rendered her decision in June of 2000, Ms. Vickers had yet to make an effort to comply with this order. I began pressing for a contempt of court hearing in December of 2000 and it took me nearly three months to get her into court, and then the judge refused to give any real direction. The judge only said that Ms. Vickers should "try harder to comply" and there was no official order issued. I was naturally in shock and angry. If the judge was not going to enforce compliance on this specific issue, then how can the judge enforce *any* issues within the decree?

Ms. Vickers continued to put her toe over every line drawn by myself, the presiding judge, or what was contained in the divorce decree. She would visit my son at his daycare when it was not authorized. She would show up at his school to pick him up when it was not authorized. She would even pick up my recycled paper at curbside to go through my trash! Police reports she filed in April of 2001 indicate that in January and February of 2001 she may have used her contacts in real estate to look at my personal things when my house was for sale and there was a lock box on the door—I had changed the locks after she moved out in June of 2000.

April 2001

On April 6, 2001, the Albany Police Department told Ms. Vickers that her complaint regarding my leaving Oregon State was a civil matter and not a criminal one. On April 9, 2001, Ms. Vickers filed a police report stating that I had interfered with her custody of my son, Michael. By divorce decree I had physical and legal custody of my son. We did not have joint custody. She only had visitation. **(Attachment B-1 through B-3)**

Testimony during the divorce proceedings in January of 2000 revealed that Ms. Vickers and her accomplice, Kimberly Dunn, acquired the name, address, telephone number, and Email address of Lisa Jergins, who is now my wife. Under testimony, Kimberly Dunn first denied, then three weeks later under oath (in court), admitted writing and mailing a letter to Lisa in August of 1999. On several occasions during the divorce proceedings in court and in statements submitted to the court, Ms. Vickers and her attorney of record, Mr. Gary Norman, knew of my relationship to Lisa Jergins and conveyed their belief that I would be moving to Texas to marry Lisa Jergins.

Kimberly Dunn's Email to Private Investigator Jeff Wilson, dated April 10, 2001, states the addresses, phone numbers, and Email addresses for my father, brothers, one of my daughters, cousins, etc. **(Attachment B-5)**

Note: On March 18, 2002 Private Investigator Jeff Wilson (a former FBI agent with 28 years in law enforcement) testified in Benton County circuit court to the validity of all Emails contained as attachments to this summary. Those Emails have since been submitted as exhibits (without objection by Ms. Vickers' attorney, Pam Hediger) to the Benton County circuit court, Judge Holcomb presiding.

Kimberly Dunn's Email to Private Investigator Jeff Wilson, dated April 11, 2001, quotes from Ms. Vickers' journal: "Robert has legal custody, therefore, it is not technically custodial interference." **(Attachment B-6)**

The copy of the Private Investigator's files reveals that on April 13, 2001, Private Investigator Jeff Wilson in Eugene contracted with a Private Investigator in Dallas to locate me. Progress notes for the month of April, 2001 reveal that the Private Investigator had obtained Lisa Jergins' work and home phone numbers and addresses. He also had Lisa's Email address and her ex-husband's contact information. The Private Investigator also had addresses, phone numbers, and Email addresses for nearly *all* of my family members, cousins, and some friends from my church affiliation in Olympia, Washington. **(Attachment B-7)**

Kimberly Dunn's Email to Private Investigator Jeff Wilson, dated April 14, 2001, reveals Lisa Jergins' current address, previous address, cell phone number, home phone number, Email addresses, employer, employer address, phone number, husband's name, his address, phone number, and Email addresses. The Email further states: "the Email that Robert was using with her shows no Email from her for the past week. My hunch is that they are together (no need for Email)." **(Attachment B-8 through B-9)**

Kimberly Dunn's Email to Private Investigator Jeff Wilson dated April 16, 2001, states: "It is very important, especially until those legal papers are issued, that nothing be done down in Texas that will tip Robert or Lisa off." **(Attachment B-10)**

Private Investigator Jeff Wilson's April 18, 2001, investigation status report reveals my family and friends' addresses, phone numbers, and Email addresses, as well as a considerable amount of financial information on myself. The report also states: "photographs of Robert Carey and Michael Carey have been sent to Dallas, Texas."

At the restitution hearing on April 12, 2002, Ms. Vickers stated that the purpose of her and Ms. Dunn's trip to Dallas and Plano, Texas more than one month later on May 20, 2001, was to take pictures of Michael and me to the authorities. The Private Investigator's report and Ms. Vickers' testimony would appear to be inconsistent.

With all of this information known to her, Ms. Vickers went to the Grand Jury as the only person to testify on the matter and from her testimony alone a warrant for my arrest was issued on March 23, 2001. That warrant states that Ms. Vickers had a valid joint custody order and that taking my son, Michael, was a class B felony. Furthermore, the second charge (contempt of court) states that I "knowingly violated a joint custody order." The divorce decree did not contain a joint custody order. **(Attachment B-4)**

The divorce decree recorded August, 28, 2000 clearly states that full legal and physical custody is awarded to Robert D. Carey, Jr. There was no joint custody. There can only be joint custody if it is agreed upon by both parties. That did not happen. The judge had to decide who had custody and it was Robert D. Carey, Jr. not Ms. Vickers. **(Attachments B-17 through B-19)**

Ms. Vickers claims to have used due diligence in her attempts to contact me. She had telephone numbers, addresses, and Email addresses for my parents, siblings, Lisa Jergins, and friends. She did not use any of those means to contact me. Her contact with all utility companies for the home I sold in Albany before departing would have revealed my forwarding address as 7900 W. Shelton-Matlock Rd., Shelton, Washington 98584 (my father's address). Following her claimed "joint custody," Ms. Vickers was able to convince the Benton County District Attorney to bring felony charges against me for "knowingly violating a joint custody order." As a result of that action, the District Attorney then subpoenaed my bank records on May 4, 2001 (hand delivered by the Albany Police Department) which revealed my mailing address as 7900 W. Shelton-Matlock Rd., Shelton, Washington 98584 (my father's address). The Benton County District Attorney received this information by fax on May 8, 2001.

May 2001

I made a withdrawal of funds in the amount of $8,000 on May 3, 2001 at a Wells Fargo Bank in North Dallas, Texas (11701 Plano Rd). On May 3, 2001 (the same day as my withdrawal of funds in Dallas, Texas) Ms. Hediger met with Private Investigator Jeff Wilson (hired by Ms. Dunn) for one hour regarding information he had on my whereabouts. My bank records were subpoenaed on May 4, 2001 and faxed to the District Attorney's office on May 8, 2001. The copy of my bank statement (from the District Attorney's files) shows 7900 W. Shelton-Matlock Rd., Shelton, Washington as my mailing address. On top of what she already knew, it would appear that Ms. Vickers likely had access to this information on May 8, 2001 showing that I was in Dallas, Texas and my mailing address was in Shelton, Washington. **(Attachment B-6)**

On May 3, 2001 Private Investigator Wilson's man in Dallas, Texas had noted Lisa Jergins address as 3304 Lanarc Dr. Plano, Texas and her employer's address in Dallas, Texas. He also made a brief, drive-by observation of our home without sighting Michael or I. All of this information was given to Private Investigator Jeff Wilson by Kimberly Dunn on March 14, 2001—so the report by the Private Investigator in Dallas, Texas was only to confirm what was already known. **(Attachment B-8)**

With the information above already known to her, Ms. Vickers continued her course of action and the following was done: The Order Allowing Service by Publication was signed on May 9, 2001. Publication of a Summons was made in the *Idaho Statesman* on May 12, May 19, May 26, and June 2 of 2001. Publication of a Summons was made in the *Corvallis Gazette-Times* on May 14, May 21,

May 28, and June 4 of 2001. Affidavit of Counsel and affidavit of Bonnie Vickers were both signed and filed on May 9, 2001.

I have never lived in Idaho. My only connection to Idaho was when I dropped off a rental truck there on March 4, 2001 and picked up another one the same day. I do not have any friends or relatives in the state of Idaho. When I lived in Oregon I lived in Albany. The only newspaper that was read while I was in residence there was the *Albany Democrat Herald*. I worked in Albany and anyone that I had any measure of contact with when I left Oregon lived in Albany.

Ms. Hediger's affidavit signed May 9, 2001 indicates that personal mail cannot be delivered to me because I did not leave a forwarding address. The post office had a forwarding address beginning April 2, 2001. All closing billings from utility companies and other correspondence was continually received at that address and then forwarded on to me. That address was 7900 W. Shelton-Matlock Rd., Shelton, WA 98584 (my father's address). Contact with utility companies would have revealed the same address. The subpoena of my bank records on May 4, 2001 revealed the same address. It would appear that Ms. Hediger had access to information between May 3, 2001 (Private Investigator Wilson) and May 8, 2001 (bank records) showing I was in Dallas, Texas and my mailing address was in Shelton, Washington. Through Private Investigator Wilson, Ms. Dunn, and Ms. Vickers' legal counsel also had access to the addresses and phone numbers of other family members, friends, and Lisa Jergins. **(Attachments B-11 and B-12)**

Ms. Vickers affidavit dated May 9, 2001 states that she "diligently attempted to locate me" and sent a letter to my former address, but that that letter was returned to her. During Ms. Vickers' testimony at the restitution hearing given on February 12, 2002 she stated that Kimberly Dunn and she made airline reservations to fly to Dallas two weeks prior to their arrival on May 20, 2001. That would make their reservation date approximately May 06, 2001 (three days *prior* to signing this affidavit).

During the divorce proceedings it was revealed that Bonnie copied contents of both my computer and my safe. She also had access to my address book and the contents of my filing cabinet. From those sources she had telephone numbers, physical addresses, and Email addresses for *all* of my family members. She also had the same contact information for Lisa Jergins. It is my word against hers that I did not leave a forwarding address, but other facts reveal information contrary to this claim: In her Emails to Private Investigator Jeff Wilson in April of 2001,

Kimberly Dunn listed a number of contact addresses, phone numbers, and Email addresses for me. The post office had a forwarding address beginning April 2, 2001. All closing billings from utility companies and other correspondence was continually received at that address then forwarded on to me. That address was 7900 W. Shelton-Matlock Rd., Shelton, Washington 98584 (my father's address). Contact with utility companies would have revealed the same address. The subpoena of my bank records on May 4, 2001 revealed the same address. It would also appear that Ms. Vickers had access to information between May 3, 2001 (Private Investigator Wilson) and May 8, 2001 (bank records) showing I was in Dallas, Texas and my mailing address was in Shelton, Washington. Additionally, through Private Investigator Wilson and Ms. Dunn she had access to the addresses and phone numbers of other family members, friends, and Lisa Jergins. **(Attachments B-13 and B-14)**

Ms. Vickers arrived at Dallas-Fort Worth airport at approximately noon on May 20, 2001. She then drove twenty-five miles north to lodge at the Holiday Inn Express in Plano, Texas. This hotel is four miles due west from where I live in Plano, Texas. The charge for the hotel is dated May 21, 2001. She left sometime thereafter because the next lodging charge is on May 23, 2001 in Shreveport, Louisiana. The fuel charge is at 4 p.m. on May 22, 2001 in Shreveport. Ms. Vickers left Dallas-Fort Worth airport at 5:55 a.m. on May 23, 2001.

In a Dallas-Fort Worth metroplex of over 6 million people, it seems more than coincidental that on May 20, 2001 Ms. Vickers took lodging within four miles of where I was living with my son, Michael, my wife, and stepchildren. As proven by her bills for restitution, this is the only geographical area that Ms. Vickers actually searched.

June 2001

Ms. Hediger filed a motion for default dated June 18, 2001. At this point, Ms. Hediger had access to my forwarding address more than six weeks prior. On May 3, 2001, prior to this motion, she met with Private Investigator Jeff Wilson. Ms. Vickers' documentation submitted for restitution reveals that she had traveled to Plano, Texas four weeks prior to this motion. With all this information known to them, Ms. Hediger and Ms. Vickers continued to execute their plan.

Kimberly Dunn's Email dated May 15, 2001 states that my father, Robert Carey Sr. and Lisa Jergins are the two people most likely connected to me. If they believed this to be true, then why didn't they send letters of notification regarding change of custody to either address?

July 2001

Benton County Circuit Court Judge issues a default judgement giving Ms. Vickers legal and physical custody of my son, Michael. This action is based upon Ms. Hediger and Ms. Vickers' affidavits that they had used due diligence to contact me and I had defaulted.

At the end of July someone began contacting my Internet friends via Email addresses under the pseudonym Candace "Candy" Cane. The Email addresses could only have been garnered by Ms. Vickers and Kimberly Dunn when they entered my locked safe and took information from my computer between August and October of 1999. Ms. Vickers also broke the lock to access my bedroom in December 1999 when she was at my home visiting with my son.

By order of the court I was not present during her visits with my son, Michael, in my home. In that break-in she got the Email address for an old friend, Karen Rogers. Karen was part of our church family in Olympia, Washington and had helped care for Michael and Linda during her illness. The Emails "Candy Cane" sent related concern for Michael's being abducted by his father, directed recipients to the www.MissingKids.com web page, and solicited information from anyone having information on our whereabouts.

August 2001

Up until this time I was not aware of any legal actions that had been going on in Oregon. I received Emails from friends advising me of the Internet poster and its contents. I viewed the information and upon noting the obvious content errors I drafted a letter (**Attachment B-15**) to the Albany Police Department and Benton County District Attorney. I mailed letters to the Albany Police and Benton County District Attorney in an effort to point out the fallacy of the information posted on the www.MissingKids.com poster. I did not receive a response even though I am certain they received it because I got a copy of that letter from the DA's files.

September 2001

It appears that sometime in August or September of 2001 the FBI was brought into the picture. They tacked on a warrant stating a charge of "flight to avoid prosecution." This was predicated on the charge of custodial interference, which someone between Benton County, Oregon and Plano, Texas then called "kidnapping." I would not be aware of all these warrants until my arrest on October 9, 2001.

October 2001

I was arrested in my home in front of my three children (Michael and two stepchildren) on October 9, 2001 and taken to jail for the next four days. I was arrested on a charge of kidnapping by a warrant issued from the Benton County District Attorney and under a warrant from the FBI for flight to avoid prosecution. The next day this charge was changed to a custodial interference felony. Michael was taken into Child Protective Services custody on October 9, 2001 at approximately 6:30 p.m. Ms. Vickers did not pick him up until two days later, on October 11, 2001. (**Attachment B-16**)

Out of concern for my son and in the best interest of expediting issues for his sake, I contested extradition. I was released on bail from Collin County, Texas under a "fugitive from justice" warrant. I immediately returned to Oregon to face arraignment and booking. Before both were completed, I met with my former pastor and Ms. Vickers' current pastor, Ed Sweet. I wanted to leave some things for Pastor Sweet to pass on to Ms. Vickers to assist in Michael's care. Ms. Vickers consented to my doing so. At arraignment I was allowed to be released on my own recognizance under the stipulation that I have no contact with my son or Ms. Vickers until a custody-hearing judge allowed such.

Prior to my booking in Benton County on October 25, 2001 my attorney at the time, Robert McCann, contacted the Albany Police Department to inquire of any outstanding warrants. The Albany Police Department indicated that there were no outstanding warrants on me. At my booking in Benton County the sheriff's deputies could not find any record of arrest warrants, so they had to enter me generically. It seems odd that warrants for two charges entered six months earlier were not found in either Benton County records or in the Albany Police records.

November 2001

Ms. Vickers knew the terms of my release forbade me to have contact with her—or with my son. Yet Ms. Vickers sent me three letters on the following dates: November 2, 2001, November 9, 2001, and November 13, 2001. The intent of these letters was little more than Ms. Vickers' attempt to get a response that would jeopardize my very freedom. While proclaiming her rights under the Oregon Victim's Rights Law, she was attempting to provoke me to contact her.

I was denied access to copies of progress notes and IEP documentation for my son, Michael, by the Albany Public School district. Ms. Vickers is an employee of the Albany Public School District. The School District's attorney claimed neutrality, but was not forthcoming with requests I submitted almost weekly beginning October 30, 2001. At my first request the Benton County District Attorney, Scott Heiser, got involved by faxing copies of my arresting warrant charges and a copy of my release agreement to the attorney for the Greater Albany School district, Mr. Schultz. This was apparently done to insinuate that I should not be entitled to my request, when my request had nothing to do with my having contact with my son.

Ms. Vickers submitted approximately $6,400 in restitution bills with the restitution clerk in the Benton County District Attorney's office. This was determined in negotiations between Mr. Armstrong and my attorney, Stephen Ensor. A negotiated settlement appeared to be formed at my court appearance on November 21, 2001. The DA's office realized that they had no case on the felony charge and agreed to drop it.

I would plead "no contest" to contempt of court and, in return, all reference to the phrase "knowingly violated a joint custody agreement" would be taken out of the contempt charge. It was agreed that a hearing would take place on November 29, 2001 to confirm the pleading, and I would appear by phone with my attorney present. At the November 29 appearance the matter was continued to December 21 to allow more time for Ms. Vickers to submit restitution bill details. The bills must be verifiable "out of pocket" expenses having to do with Ms. Vickers' claim that she had expenses related to locating me and bringing Michael back to Oregon.

December 2001

On December 4, 2001 Ms. Vickers priority mailed Michael's suitcase to my home in Texas—it subsequently arrived on December 10. This appears to be in response to her being served with "contempt of court" papers and "request for custody hearing" papers. This is also an attempt to provoke me into violating my terms of release and thereby endangering my freedom. The items received in the mail from Ms. Vickers, inside Michael's own suitcase, included those things Michael personally took with him when Child Protective Services picked him up on October 9, 2001.

When I spoke with Pastor Ed Sweet on October 22, 2001, I asked him if I could leave some clothes and school books for Michael with him if it was okay with Ms Vickers. Pastor Sweet said he contacted Ms. Vickers and that the arrangement was fine with her. The next day I left three bags of things for Michael, including his third and fourth grade home school books and papers. The bags of clothing included the following:

- 1 pair of new shoes
- 1 pair of new insulated snow pants
- 1 new pair of insulated gloves
- 1 new stocking hat (with a Colorado Rockies logo that Ms. Vickers' niece gave to him for Christmas three years ago)
- 1 new insulated vest
- 1 pair swim trunks
- 2 pair black sweatpants
- 1 new pair of Scooby-Do earmuffs
- 3 pairs of white socks
- 3 white T-shirts
- 2 pairs of underwear
- 1 red logo T-shirt that he picked out
- 1 California logo T-shirt that his grandmother gave him last Christmas
- 1 baby seal stuffed toy that is a favorite of his

- 1 meerkat stuffed toy Michael picked out when we went to the Dallas zoo together in June of 2001

- 6 pictures of Michael at the Dallas zoo, Natural History Museum, Texas State Fair, and with me

- A note for Michael to let him know that I was okay, I loved him, and I hoped to talk to him sometime soon, and also containing my phone number; a message that his toys and things were safe with me; and also telling him to be good, be happy, and I was going to pray for him every day

Also in the suitcase were some things that Michael picked out that he specifically wanted to take with him when Child Protective Services picked him up:

- 1 Dalmatian stuffed toy dog that was given to him right after his mother died when he was 2-years-old

- 1 stuffed blue puppy dog toy that he won when he went with me to the Texas State Fair in September of 2001

- 1 stuffed shark toy that he picked out when I took him to the Oregon coast aquarium on a second grade field trip

- 8 of his favorite action figure toys

All of the above things were taken away from Michael and mailed to me in his own suitcase. (**Attachment D-10**)

On December 12, 2001 the attorney for the Albany Public School district mailed me a few notes for a meeting that took place on November 28, 2001. He did *not* send me any of the other copies, as I'd requested, and through the end of this month did not respond to any of my correspondence.

On December 24, 2001 I received in the mail from Ms. Vickers a box containing Michael's home school curriculum books, notebooks, and monthly progress notes—all from the six full months in which I home schooled him under Texas State law. Before I was arraigned and booked in Benton County, I left these things with Ms. Vickers' pastor after receiving her permission to do so. My intent was to assist the school district in their assessment for developing an Individual Education Plan for my son, Michael. During my request for documentation with the school district, I asked if they had seen this documentation. No one with the school district provided me any verification that they had done so.

On December 18, 2001 Ms. Hediger submitted an incomplete listing of restitution documentation. This was three days prior to the court date, and she apparently indicated that she would be on vacation and not available until after the New Year. The total went from $6,400 to $15,880. Less than one-fourth of this amount had verifiable information. The District Attorney asked for more time to contact Ms. Hediger and get the verifiable documentation. The matter was continued until January 15, 2002.

January 2002

At 4 p.m. on Friday, January 10, 2002 Ms. Hediger's office faxed a detailed invoice for her office's attorney fees beginning with March 20, 2001 through January 9, 2002. The rest of the requested documentation was not submitted to the DA's office *nor* to my attorney's office. The attorney billings began on March 20, 2001 while I was still in my Albany residence and *before* Ms. Vickers signed the closing papers for my house in Albany, Oregon.

At the January 15, 2002 court appearance—I was still authorized by the court to appear by telephone—the matter was continued once again to January 28, 2002. The District Attorney did not want to take a pleading/sentencing until we had full agreement on the amount of restitution. This time was to allow the DA an additional two weeks to get the required restitution documentation for verification.

On January 20, 2002 I received a near complete response from Albany School District principal Ric Blasquez. I was still requesting confirmation that someone on the team actually reviewed the home school related documentation that I had left to assist in the development of Michael's IEP. The question remained as to why the school district took ten weeks to give an adequate response to my request of October 30, 2001. Why would they withhold information that is clearly within my rights as a parent to obtain?

At the January 28, 2002 court date, the felony charge was officially dropped. On the paperwork the DA states: "no contact with son, Michael Carey, unless approved by court in pending dissolution case." The divorce was granted and recorded nearly 18 months prior to this date. I had full custody out of that divorce. Ms. Vickers got custody by default after a number of fraudulent actions on her part. What was "pending" was a change of custody hearing where I was asking that custody be given back to me based upon the fraud that had been committed by Ms. Vickers. (**Attachments B-20 and B-21**)

February 2002

At the restitution hearing on February 12, 2001, the judge dropped the amount from a figure close to $15,000 down to $9,800. The protracted delays in this matter were deliberate on the part of Ms. Vickers in order to manipulate the system and deny my son access to his father and his family. A custody hearing would not take place until the pleadings and restitution were addressed. Ms. Vickers deliberately made this last as long as she could. Meanwhile, my son was held hostage by what amounted to little more than extortion.

March 2002

On March 18, 2002 the custody hearing process would begin and I was finally given visitation rights with my son. More importantly, my son could now talk to me after being denied that right for more than six months! If anyone was a victim in all of this mess, it is Michael Carey. His only living biological parent and primary care provider for the first nine and a half years of his life was ripped out of his life by way of fraud and malicious actions on the part of Ms. Vickers.

Ms. Vickers' facade of lies and misinformation continued as she took Michael to Oregon Health Science University on March 1, 2002 under the guise of getting a current medical diagnosis for autism. The reported interview background information as reflected in the content of this report reveals how Ms. Vickers would have it be something more than a diagnostic tool. Instead, it is an attempt on her part to lend credibility to her fraud.

According to the report, she indicated that my son was abducted from her custody, which is a blatant lie. Obviously, Michael was present at this interview so once again he was subjected to hearing a lot of lies and misinformation about his father. He was in no position to be able to do anything but tolerate her words. The flavor of the report is such that conclusions are drawn from the foundation of her lies. Ms. Vickers provides numerous other false details that predate her involvement in Michael's life. Unfortunately, this report is now in my son's educational file and would appear to have authority by way of the credentials of the disciplinarian doctors. The audacity of Ms. Vickers knows no boundaries. She seems to be operating on the premise that her desired end justifies any and all means. (**Attachments B-22 through B-24**)

June 2002

The change of custody hearing was continued to May 15th, 2002 and then onto June 19th and 21st. On June 19th, Ms. Kimberly Dunn was asked if she knew where Michael and Robert had gone after they left Albany on April 2, 2001. She said that she did not have any idea. The documentation would indicate otherwise (**Attachments B-5, B-8, and B-9**).

Ms. Dunn was asked about **Attachment B-6**, which is an Email she wrote to Private Investigator Wilson on March 11, 2001. She quoted Ms. Vickers as writing: "the downside is that R has legal custody, therefore it is not technically custodial interference." Ms. Dunn was asked if she discussed this situation with Ms. Vickers, to which she replied that she did not recall. Ms. Dunn was also asked when she and Ms. Vickers picked up Michael after I was arrested on the charge of kidnapping reduced to custodial interference. She said they picked up Michael about noon on October 10, 2001. Yet the ticket stub provided for restitution shows that they did not arrive in Dallas until 10:53 p.m. on October 10th, so there is no way they could have picked Michael up until the 11th. He was in CPS custody in a strange environment, away from his father and not knowing what would happen to him for nearly two days.

On June 21, 2002, the final day of testimony, Ms. Vickers was asked if she realized that Mr. Carey had legal and physical custody of Michael at the time she filed a police report stating that Mr. Carey had committed custodial interference (**Attachments B-1 through B-3**). She said she did not know the procedures or legal terms. She said she was just following the lead of the authorities in the legal system. When asked what she told the District Attorney, she said she did not recall and did not understand the procedures. When asked if she had legal counsel before going to the police with her claim of custodial interference, she said she could not remember. When confronted with a copy of her attorney's itemized billings showing she clearly *had* talked to her attorney on several occasions before going to the police, only then did her attorney concede that Ms. Vickers was under legal counsel at the time she went to the DA and the police. When asked if she told the grand jury that she had joint custody, she said she did not remember.

She *did* remember that she was the only person to testify to the grand jury. When asked why she didn't tell someone that the indictment was incorrect in stating that Mr. Carey had committed custodial interference, she said she did not understand what the procedure was. When asked if she was happy when the grand jury came down with an indictment that would lead to the felony arrest of Mr. Carey, she finally had to admit that she was.

In regard to the affidavit Ms. Vickers signed on May 9, 2001 in which she claimed to have used due diligence in trying to contact Mr. Carey, she was asked why she did not utilize the addresses that she and Kimberly Dunn had given to Private Investigator Wilson. She had no answer. When asked why she chose to advertise in the Corvallis and Boise, Idaho newspapers when Emails show that she suspected that Mr. Carey was in Dallas, Texas and was in contact with his father and Lisa Jergins, she claimed she was not certain that Mr. Carey was not in Boise, Idaho. When asked why she did not advertise in the newspaper where Mr. Carey's father resides—Shelton, Washington—or in the newspaper where Lisa Jergins lives—Plano, Texas—she had no answer. When asked if she checked to see if there was a newspaper in either place she said, "No."

Ms. Vickers was asked if she knew that the felony charge against Mr. Carey had been dropped. She said she did not remember. When asked if she had received restitution for her expenses, which she had claimed in her complaint against Mr. Carey, she said she had more expenses than what had been paid. She claims to have additional travel and legal expenses that had not been paid for. The court was advised that there was a restitution hearing and Ms. Vickers had been given full restitution for all reasonable expenses that she had submitted.

Ms. Vickers had by now raised so many lies that the judge seemed compelled to let her run out her allegations to avoid any potential of an appeal! The biggest lie began on April 9, 2001 when Ms. Vickers claimed custodial interference. On the police report she said she was the person reporting. So how can she be a victim? She claimed Michael's address and phone number are the same as her address and phone number. His last Albany address was the same as his father's last Albany address: 1450 NW Patrick Lane and the phone number for both Michael and his father was 926-6453. She claimed that *Michael* was the victim. How can Michael be a victim when he was in the legal and physical custody of his father? (**Attachments B-1 through B-3**)

Things only got worse from there as Ms. Vickers had to perpetuate the lie in order to get her desired end result. In order to get what she never had in the first place, she had to lie and be convincing enough so that the authorities would be forced to believe her lie. Even after the felony charge was dropped officially in January of 2002, Ms. Vickers continued the lie when on March 1, 2002 she went to OHSU—CDRC under the guise of getting a medical diagnosis of autism for Michael (**Attachments B-22 through B-24**).

Three doctors on two separate reports recount her claim that she had joint custody, and primary responsibility for Michael after the divorce and that Mr. Carey had abducted Michael from her care. There were five component reports to the evaluation that had numerous lies and incorrect background information, which was supplied by Ms. Vickers. Ms. Vickers made no attempt to inform me of this report until *after* it was issued, so that there would be no opportunity for me to give input. Ms. Vickers then made this document a part of Michael's educational file.

Note: While in Albany, Oregon on June 18th, I went to the Albany Police Department to file a police report regarding the false police report Ms. Vickers had filed in April of 2001. They kept me waiting for more than 90 minutes to talk to the sergeant. He would take my report, but would not read it or look at the documentation attached to this summary. He gave it back to me saying that "the Benton County DA had closed this file and the Albany Police would not open it unless the DA *directed* them to open it." I advised my attorney of these events, and he was not surprised. He said: "facts are less important than they might seem. The DA normally chooses which side of an issue he will come down on, and he is not likely to change his mind thereafter." I instructed my attorney to at least *try* to have the DA look at these documents that clearly show that Bonnie both lied *and* used him.

APPENDIX B

The Evidence

The following documents pertain to the unbelievable events that took place between April 2001 and March 2002. I have also enclosed pertinent elements of the original divorce decree, to further your understanding of the "letter of the law" pertaining to this particular case. These numbered pages can be correlated to the parenthetical references found in the preceding chronology of events (*Appendix A*).

ALBANY POLICE   ☒ 008

ALBANY POLICE DEPARTMENT

CASE NO. _____
OFFICE USE ONLY

Referred by Capt. McLain
CRIME REPORTING INFORMATION

PLEASE PRINT

YOUR NAME: Vickers (Carey)   Bonnie   Joann
            Last   *First*   *Middle*

YOUR ADDRESS: 1830 NW Thornton Lake Pl, Albany, OR 97321
                                      City   *State* *Zip*

YOUR PHONE #: 926-8355   967-4578   DATE OF BIRTH: 11/23/50
              Home #   *Work #*   *Month/Day/Year*

ARE YOU THE VICTIM OF THIS INCIDENT?   X YES   ____ NO

ADDRESS WHERE INCIDENT OCCURRED: 1450 NW Patrick Lane

DATE & TIME INCIDENT OCCURRED *(Estimate)*: 5:00 Monday to current

TYPE OF INCIDENT (criminal mischief, hit & run, harassment, traffic violation, etc): ____
Custodial Interference

BRIEFLY DESCRIBE INCIDENT: I was to pick up my son, Michael, at
5:00 April 1, Monday. I confirmed that with his dad at 12:30
that afternoon. When I got to the house, it was cleaned out and
no one showed. Robert Carey had picked up Michael at school at 2:15.
They have not been seen face since. Robert had a Ryder truck that he
listed would be turned in at Oregon City. It was turned in at Boise, Ida
on Tuesday, April 3. He is in violation of at least 4 pts of the dissolution decr

IF YOU HAVE INFORMATION ABOUT A SUSPECT OR YOU ARE NOT THE VICTIM, PLEASE
COMPLETE THE FOLLOWING INFORMATION:
                                    might use alias of Rob Johnson
SUSPECT/~~VICTIM~~ NAME: Carey   Jr. Robert   Dean
                         Last   *First*   *Middle*

SUSPECT/~~VICTIM~~ ADDRESS: moved from 1450 NW Patrick Lane, Albany, OR.
                                        City   *State* *Zip*
                 formerly 926-6453 H
SUSPECT/VICTIM PHONE: 917-4829 W   DATE OF BIRTH: 2/8/49
                      no 0770 cell
VEHICLE INVOLVED: Ryder Truck he had a 1984 Honda Civic blue DTU 499
                  Make   *Model*   *Color*   *License #*

WAS VEHICLE LOCKED?   ____ YES   NO

VEHICLE WAS PARKED IN (Circle One):   Street   Driveway   Parking Lot   Other

A 73 · *September 16, 1997*

B-1

SUPPLEMENTAL REPORT

BONNIE VICKERS told me she contacted her lawyer, who advised her to wait until 04/06/01, and if no contact was made, to report this incident to the Court and the police. She told me she contacted the Albany Police Department on 04/06/01 to report the incident. She told me she was advised this incident was a civil matter, not a criminal one.

Robert CAREY JR's actions appear to have violated the divorce decree. Section 2.2 stipulates "until further notice of the Court, Respondent's residence must be within sixty (60) miles of Petitioner's current residence to facilitate Petitioner's parenting time with Michael. Also, the visitation requirements appear to have been violated.   *counter*

ACTION RECOMMENDED:

Forward to the Benton County District Attorney's Office, Attention: Scott Heiser.

Reporting Officer	DPSST#	Shift:	Assignment	Supervisor Approval:
Kevin P. Manske	31827	Patrol		

Suspect Supplemental Report

led

APR 2 5 2001
Ben... ....., Circuit Court
Corvallis, Oregon

1

IN THE CIRCUIT COURT OF THE STATE OF OREGON
FOR THE COUNTY OF BENTON

2

STATE OF OREGON,   )
          Plaintiff,   )   INDICTMENT   Entered _____

3

vs.   )
)   Court No.   CMO120629

4

ROBERT DEAN CAREY,   )
          Defendant   )

5

The Defendant is accused by the Grand Jury for Benton County of the following offenses:

6

Count 1:   CUSTODIAL INTERFERENCE IN THE FIRST DEGREE (FSG=6; B Felony; ORS 163.257)

7
FPC#:

8
Count 2:   CONTEMPT OF COURT (U Misdemeanor; ORS 033.015) FPC#:

committed as follows:

9
COUNT 1

10
The defendant, on or about April 9, 2001, in the County of Benton, State of Oregon, knowing, or having reason to
know that the defendant had no legal right to do so, took, enticed and kept Michael Carey from Bonnie Vickers, a
person having a valid joint custody order, with intent to hold Michael Carey for a protracted period. The State

11
further alleges that the defendant caused Michael Carey to be removed from the State of Oregon.

12
COUNT 2

13
The defendant, on or about April 9, 2001, in the County of Benton, State of Oregon, did unlawfully and knowingly
violate a valid joint custody order, dated August 28, 2000, of the Benton County Circuit Court.

14
WITNESSES: A TRUE BILL.
Bonnie Vickers

15
                            Grand Jury Foreperson

16
                            SCOTT A. HEISER
                            DISTRICT ATTORNEY

17
                            By _____

18
                            Daniel C Armstrong
                            Deputy District Attorney
                            Oregon State Bar No. 88151

19
                            DATE: April 23, 2001

20
A warrant to be issued with   CLERK'S CERTIFICATE
Security in the amount of   I hereby certify this copy to

21
                        be a true, full and correct
S _____   copy of the original now on
                        record in my office.

22
DATE: _____

23
                          Clerk of the Circuit Court
                          by: _____
                            Deputy

24
Judge
Page 1 – INDICTMENT

Benton County District Attorney
120 NW Fourth Street
Corvallis Oregon 97330 (541) 766-6815

SECRET

MSN Home Hotmail Web Search Shopping Money People & Chat

msn

Hotmail jwilso1@hotmail.com

Inbox   Compose   Address Book   Folders   Options   Messenger   Calendar   Help

Folder: Inbox

From: "Kimberly Dunn" <kdunn@welcomehomeloans.com> Save Address - Block Sender
To: <JWILSO1@hotmail.com> Save Address
Subject: friends &family
Date: Tue, 10 Apr 2001 18:50:01 -0700

Reply   Reply All   Forward   Delete   Previous   Next   Close

Family and Friends
Bob&Nancy Carey (Father and step-mother)360-426-6558, 7900 W. Shelton-Matlock Rd., Shelton, WA 98584.e-mail BCandNC@aol.com Robert keeps in contact with them. Robert's father testified (lied) for him in court.

Chuck Carey (brother)425-820-9919, 12041 87th Ave. N.E., Kirkland, WA, 98034. Charlescarey@aol.com, C2CAREY@aol.com Robert keeps in touch with Chuck. I would consider Chuck to be pretty loyal to Robert, but maybe less if he knew Robert had lied and broken the law. I believe Chuck is currently stated as the executor of Robert's will and has power of attorney should anything happen.

Sylvie Carey (mother)714-774-4874. Robert keeps in touch with Sylvie, but I doubt he would give her any info. regarding his whereabouts. He may tell her that he is on vacation somewhere though.

Shannon Finnessey (daughter from first wife Sarah)413-527-1308, 1 Susan Drive, Easthampton, MA, 01027. snf1974@aol.com. Shannon is in good standing with Robert, but I doubt he would let her know right away where he is at. He may tell in the form of being on an extended vacation though.

Joseph Carey (brother)lives in Seattle/Olympia area.

Brian David Carey (half-brother lives in Seattle/Olympia area.

Susan Wheeler (half sister lives in Seattle/Olympia area.)milvandersan1995@yahoo.com

Kim Thayer (daughter from first wife, Sarah)We have been in contact with Kim. She hates Robert and has not had a relationship with him. Robert would not contact her, and if he did, she would let us know. She lives in Mass. like her younger sister, Shannon.

Debbie and Fred Russell (friends from Church Robert went to when he lived in Olympia 7 years ago, Robert has kept in touch and probably somewhat updated on the events of his divorce)FRuss73680@aol.com, 1700 Foxfire Drive S.E., Olympia, WA, 98513, 360-491-6022.

Karen Rogers (also a friend from Robert's old Church)stuffit@home.com, 13100Riley Rd. S., Olympia, WA 98512, 360-357-5299. Robert has also kept in touch with Karen. She also testified for Robert during the divorce. Robert has his Church friends thinking that he is an innocent victim and upstanding christian. They would probably be surprised if they heard he has broken the law.

Ruth Libbey (can't remember if this is a friend or a relative) libbysinn@cs.com.

Reply   Reply All   Forward   Delete   Previous   Next   Close

.../getmsg?curmbox=F00000000l&a=1877f620eb28c3e18b44e5383la3da2a&msg=MSG987016 4/11/01

Hotmail Folder: Inbox

Folder: Inbox

From: "Kimberly Dunn" <kdunn@welcomehomeloans.com> Save Address - Block Sender
To: "Jeff Wilson" <jwilso1@hotmail.com> Save Address
Subject: Re: friends & family
Date: Wed, 11 Apr 2001 19:21:04 -0700
Reply   Reply All   Forward   Delete   Previous   Next   Close

Jeff,
Bonnie and I journal and keep notes of things as they occur. I am
forwarding this to you (Bonnie's journal) as I thought it will help keep you
up to speed on the process.
Kimberly
Journal 4/11/01

 I talked to Scott Heiser from the Benton County DA's office.
(541-766-6815) He seemed to want to be helpful and was straight forward.
He is passing this case to Dan Armstrong to be the prosecutor. Dan will
take this to the Grand Jury in three or four days. The down side is that R
has legal custody, therefore it is not technically custodial interference.
Scott said that R is clearly in contempt of court. The up side is that I
was given certain rights the same as R's as far as Michael's
life--education, legal, medical, psychological, etc. He said that is a
small peg to hang our hat on, but we can hope.
 I told him that I had a lawyer and that we filed papers yesterday. When I
told him that the lawyer was Pam Hediger, he said that she is a good
attorney and used to work in the DA's office. I told him that we filed the
Motions of Contempt and for emergency custody. He said, 'Perfect' in an
excited way. He said that if I get custody, then they can act on charging R
and finding him with legal forces. Scott was going to call P H right away.
He hopes this action by the judge is taken before the Grand Jury meets. He
seemed sympathetic to our cause.

 I am going to call Albany Police today and ask for a copy of the report
they filed with the DA's office.

Reply   Reply All   Forward   Delete   Previous   Next   Close

Move To [(Move to Selected Folder) ▾]

.../getmsg?curmbox=F000000001&a=2c238fc4024c0eb1b9dc6a529ada7cf9&msg=MSG98704214/11/01

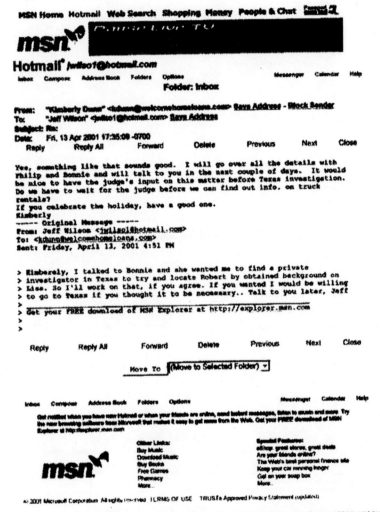

Hotmail Folder: Inbox

MSN Home Hotmail Web Search Shopping Money People & Chat

Hotmail jwilso1@hotmail.com

Inbox Compose Address Book Folders Options   Messenger Calendar Help

Folder: Inbox

From: "Kimberly Dunn" <kdunn@welcomehomeloans.com> Save Address - Block Sender
To: "Jeff Wilson" <jwilso1@hotmail.com> Save Address
Subject: Re:
Date: Fri, 13 Apr 2001 17:35:09 -0700

Reply   Reply All   Forward   Delete   Previous   Next   Close

Yes, something like that sounds good. I will go over all the details with
Philip and Bonnie and will talk to you in the next couple of days. It would
be nice to have the judge's input on this matter before Texas investigation.
Do we have to wait for the judge before we can find out info. on truck
rentals?
If you celebrate the holiday, have a good one.
Kimberly
------ Original Message -----
From: Jeff Wilson <jwilso1@hotmail.com>
To: <kdunn@welcomehomeloans.com>
Sent: Friday, April 13, 2001 4:51 PM

> Kimberely, I talked to Bonnie and she wanted me to find a private
> investigator in Texas to try and locate Robert by obtained background on
> Lisa. So I'll work on that, if you agree. If you wanted I would be willing
> to go to Texas if you thought it to be necessary.. Talk to you later, Jeff
>
> _____
> Get your FREE download of MSN Explorer at http://explorer.msn.com
>
>

Reply   Reply All   Forward   Delete   Previous   Next   Close

Move To [(Move to Selected Folder) ▼]

Inbox Compose Address Book Folders Options   Messenger Calendar Help

Get notified when you have new Hotmail or when your friends are online, send instant messages, listen to music and more. Try
the new browsing software from Microsoft that makes it easy to get news from the Web. Get your FREE download of MSN
Explorer at http://explorer.msn.com

Other Links: Special Features:
Buy Music   eShop: great stores, great deals
Download Music   Are your friends online?
Buy Books   The Web's best personal finance site
Free Games   Keep your car running longer
Pharmacy   Get on your soap box
More...   More...

.../getmsg?curmbox=F000000001&a=cc7909bb449164cd9b29c9f7b19042e1&msg=MSG987208 4/13/01

HOTMAIL FOLDER: INBOX

MSN Home Hotmail Web Search Shopping Money People & Chat

msn

Hotmail jwilso1@hotmail.com

Inbox Compose Address Book Folders Options   Messenger Calendar Help

Folder: Inbox

From: "Kimberly Dunn" <kdunn@welcomehomeloans.com> Save Address - Block Sender
To: "Jeff Wilson" <jwilso1@hotmail.com> Save Address
Subject: update
Date: Sat, 14 Apr 2001 18:40:03 -0700

Reply   Reply All   Forward   Delete   Previous   Next   Close

Jeff,
I have an updated information list on Lisa Jergins (exxas girlfriend). Bonnie, Philip and I will be meeting today to see what is the best to further investigate this avenue. I'll get back to you by Monday.
Kimberly

Lisa Kay Jergins, (other name used, Melies)DOB:12-21-55, height:5'6".

Most current address: 3304 Lenarc Drive, Plano, TX 75023-8112 (Collin County)

Previous address: 4206 San Gabriel Drive, Plano, TX 75229.

personal numbers: mobile: 214-354-4406.

home?:469-467-8070

e-mail:peach_1221@yahoo.com, peach_1221@hotmail.com

Recently divorced to Allan Jergins (within last two years) Allen's most current address could be 9794 Forest Ln. #125, Dallas, TX, 75243, but internet also lists 4206 San Gabriel Drive (where he lived with Lisa)

Allen's phone:214-902-9133.

Allen's e-mail: JackpotJer@aol.com, jackpotjer2@aol.com

I believe they have two school age children together, Shannon and Derek.

Lisa'sEmployment: Works as a property accountant.

Genesis Realty incorporated

5710 Lyndon B Johnson Fwy. #348 (or #328), Dallas, TX 75240

General phone: 972-404-8208

.../getmsg?curmbox=F000000001&a=f3052dbdc8bbfe547d8e15111c9c5ba0&msg=MSG987270 4/14/01

B-8

Hotmail Folder: INBOX

Voicemail/personal extension: 972-404-8288 ext. 178

M.Jergins@agenesis.org

Distance between home and work is 11.5 miles. Have copy of directions from Mapquest.

Notes: During the first week after Michael was missing, I called Lisa's work number and personal extension. got her voicemail. On April 15, I called the number again. She had updated her voicemail that said she would be in the office until noon and then back on Monday.

Lisa and Robert would communicate daily via e-mail. The e-mail that Robert was using with her shows no e-mails from her for the past week. My hunch is they are either together (no need for e-mail) or communicating via another mailbox (maybe the hushmail).

Lisa's home address is in Collin County, we might want to check for any recent marriage licenses. County clerk for Collin Co. is Helen Starnes: 972-548-4134.

Other counties nearby:

Denton:940-565-8686, Rockwall:972-882-0340, Dallas:214-653-7565.

I'm pretty sure Lisa is renting. I know her and her former husband were having financial problems, hadn't filed last year's tax returns. Lisa also may have or is currently going through bankruptcy (public record?). It might be possible to find out the owner of the property she is renting and get some info. from him/her (such as mo. to mo./or lease, still there?,etc.)I don't think Robert will buy a house right away.

What schools (public and private) are near home address.

Churches close by? I'm pretty sure Lisa attends church and her and Robert talk about the bible. It is very possible that they will go to church together.

Contacting Allen? He may be able to give us a lot of info. as he has children with Lisa. He may be concerned about the person Lisa is getting involved with (someone who likes teenage girls).

Vehicles licensed in her name?

Reply   Reply All   Forward   Delete   Previous   Next   Close

...Jgetmsg?curmbox=F000000001&a=f3052dbde8bbfc547d8e15111c9e3ba0&msg=MSG987270 4/14/01

Hotmail Folder: Inbox

Folder: Inbox

From: "Kimberly Dunn" <kdunn@brokennahomeloans.com> **Save Address - Block Sender**
To: "Jeff Wilson" <jwilso1@hotmail.com> **Save Address**
Subject: Re: Good morning
Date: Mon, 16 Apr 2001 12:11:53 -0700

Reply   Reply All   Forward   Delete   Previous   Next   Close

Hi Jeff,
Yes, we want to get someone started on finding out the situation down there.
We would like someone who is retired FBI like yourself, or has a lot of
experience following and finding people and comes with good recommendation.
Knowing the Dallas/Plano area is also a good thing. As far as I know, we
have not heard back from the judge yet regarding change of custody. It is
my understanding that when Bonnie receives emergency custody, we can have
more help from law enforcement. Since she doesn't have that yet, I think we
would to have the investigator in Texas nail down the facts we have on Lisa
Jergins, like verifying that she still is living at the address we have for
her, still working at Genesis Realty. Also maybe checking Collin county
records for any recent marriage licenses for her and Robert. We don't have
any photos of her, only a video that has a small clip of her in it. Bonnie
has seen a photo of her and her kids in Robert's safe, but she did not keep
it. In addition to seeing if Robert is with Lisa, here are some of the
things we thought would be helpful to know.
Vehicle information (make,color, model, plate #)
What schools close by to residence (public and private)
What schools do her kids go to.
What churches close by. She may go to church on Sunday, what church?
Is she still currently working at Genesis Real Estate?
Anything else that we aren't thinking of that would be helpful?

My understanding of this procedure is, when Bonnie gets emergency custody,
we will need to have Robert physically served with papers for custody and
for contempt. At the same time, Michael will need to be removed from Robert
by a county sheriff. Philip and I may also have papers that we want served
to him as well. It is very important, especially until those legal papers
are issued, that nothing is done down in Texas that will tip Robert or Lisa
off. So talking to her or her x-husband at this point or anybody else
related to them would not be a good idea.

Let me know if you have any questions or comments about this. I have one
other little discovery/idea that I will mail to you in another e-mail.
Thanks
Kimberly

----- Original Message -----
From: Jeff Wilson <jwilso1@hotmail.com>

http://lw8fd.law8.hotmail.msn.com/cgi-bin/getmsg?curmbox=F000000001&a=c17b39fe28c016 4/16/01

1

2

3

4

IN THE CIRCUIT COURT OF THE STATE OF OREGON

5

FOR THE COUNTY OF BENTON

6

7   In the Matter of the Marriage of   )
)   Case No. 99-30362
8   BONNIE J. CAREY, nka   )
     BONNIE J. VICKERS, Petitioner,   )   **AFFIDAVIT OF COUNSEL**
9   )
)
10   and   )
)
11   ROBERT D. CAREY, JR., Respondent.)

12   STATE OF OREGON   )
)   ss.
13   County of Benton   )

14   I, PAMELA S. HEDIGER, after first being duly sworn, do depose and say as

15   follows:

16   1.   That I am the attorney for the petitioner, Bonnie J. Vickers, in the

17   above-referenced matter.

18

19   2.   I attempted to serve the summons in this matter on respondent

20   through his attorney of record, Robert McCann, but Mr. McCann indicated that he

21   no longer represents respondent and cannot accept service. A copy of Mr.

22   McCann's letter and enclosures is attached hereto and incorporated herein by this

23   reference as Exhibit A.

24   3.   Neither personal nor mail service can be made on respondent

25   because he has moved without leaving a forwarding address.

26

PAGE 1 - AFFIDAVIT OF COUNSEL
      Vickers v. Carey

1   4.   Respondent is not employed so he cannot be served through office

2   service.

3   5.   Respondent rented a Ryder truck to move his personal property and

4   information obtained by petitioner is that the truck was returned in Boise, Idaho. The

5   newspaper of general circulation in Boise is the Idaho Statesman.

6

7   DATED this 9th day of May, 2001.

8   _____
     PAMELA S. HEDIGER - #91309

9

10   Subscribed and sworn to before me this ___ day of May, 2001.

11   _____
      NOTARY PUBLIC FOR OREGON

12
      OFFICIAL SEAL
13   DEBORAH G. SEELEY
      NOTARY PUBLIC-OREGON
      COMMISSION NO. 339846
14   MY COMMISSION EXPIRES NOV. 3, 2004

15

16

17

18

19

20

21

22

23

24

25

26

745 N.W. VAN BUREN • P.O. BOX 791
CORVALLIS, OR 97339
(541) 754-0303

PAGE 2 - AFFIDAVIT OF COUNSEL
Vickers v. Carey

1

2

3

4   IN THE CIRCUIT COURT OF THE STATE OF OREGON

5

6   FOR THE COUNTY OF BENTON

7   In the Matter of the Marriage of   )
)   Case No. 99-30362
8   BONNIE J. CAREY, nka   )
     BONNIE J. VICKERS, Petitioner,   )   **AFFIDAVIT OF BONNIE VICKERS**
9   )
)
10   and   )
)
11   ROBERT D. CAREY, JR., Respondent.)

12   STATE OF OREGON   )
)   ss.
13   County of Benton   )

14   I, BONNIE J. VICKERS, formerly known as Bonnie J. Carey, after first being

15   duly sworn, do depose and say as follows:

16   1. That I am the psychological mother of MICHAEL ROBERT CAREY and the

17   ex-wife of respondent, ROBERT D. CAREY, JR., Michael's father.

18

19   2.   That the information contained in the Motion for Show Cause re.

20   Remedial Contempt and my affidavit in support of the Motion is true and correct.

21   3.   That I have attempted to obtain respondent's current address by

22   mailing a letter to respondent's last known address and that the letter came back

23   to me from the post office stamped "temporarily away return to sender."

24   4.   I have diligently attempted to locate respondent, including hiring a

25   private investigator for that purpose, but have had no success in doing so.

26

     Page 1 - AFFIDAVIT OF BONNIE VICKERS
         Vickers v. Carey

                                    B-13

FILED

MAY - 9 2001

BENTON COUNTY COURTS
BENTON COUNTY, OREGON

1 5.   I make this Affidavit in support of my attorney's motion to allow service by

2 publication.

3

4 DATED this 9th day of May, 2001.

5

6   BONNIE J. VICKERS

7 Subscribed and sworn to before me this 9th day of May, 2001.

8

9   NOTARY PUBLIC FOR OREGON

10   OFFICIAL SEAL
        DEBORAH G. SEELEY
        NOTARY PUBLIC-OREGON
        COMMISSION NO. 339846
11   MY COMMISSION EXPIRES NOV 3, 2004

12

13

14

15

16

17

18

19

20

21

22

23

24

25

26

745 N.W. VAN BUREN • P.O. BOX 781
CORVALLIS, OR 97339
(541) 754-0303

Page 2 - AFFIDAVIT OF BONNIE VICKERS
        Vickers v Carey

Robert D. Carey, Jr.
7900 W. Shelton-Matlock Rd.
Shelton, WA 98584
360-426-6556

August 02, 2001

To Whom it may concern,

I am writing in regards to a very damaging lie that you have been party to. You have been deceived and the lie has snowballed. I am including copies of legal documents that you can verify with originals from the proper legal authorities in Oregon and Washington. It is my understanding that you have not seen these documents but have gone on the assumption that the affidavit of facts accompanying a missing person report filed by Ms. Vickers was truthful. This missing person report was then used as the basis for issuing a warrant for my arrest under the pretext that I was not the custodial parent of Michael and that I had abducted Michael. The warrant was then used as a basis for getting "Missing Kids" to certify the facts of the case and issuing a poster over the internet.

Please be advised that my ex-wife, Bonnie Joann Vickers and her accomplice, Kimberly Ann Dunn, have proven themselves to be perjurious liars. A thorough review of the facts, testimony and documentation in the divorce case will reveal their lies. They made several affidavits during the divorce case in an attempt to add weight to their dubious theories. They also admitted to lying in court testimony. Outside of the courtroom they have made every conceivable attempt to smear, slander and harass me (including their refusal to return stolen documentation they took from my personal safe). Ms. Vickers abused her authority as a teacher in attempting to use her influence to pressure people into providing her with confidential information and at the same time pressuring people to withhold information from me. She appears to have used her position in the community to add weight to the purported validity of her lies.

Point #1 (see divorce decree)
Judge Holcomb in Benton County presided over this divorce and in the accompanying decree you can clearly see that I, Robert D. Carey, Jr., was awarded full custody of my son, Michael R. Carey. Judge Holcomb's decision was based upon the obvious: I have been primary care giver for my son, Michael R. Carey, since his mother, Linda S. Carey, got sick from the effects of cancer treatment and died. I stayed home with Michael full time while Ms. Vickers worked outside the home full time.

Point #2 (see birth certificate for Michael and death certificate for Linda Carey)
As you can see Michael's birth parents are myself and Linda S. Carey who died June 4, 1994. Ms Vickers never knew my son until he was 2 and 1/2 yrs old. Ms. Vickers did not give birth to Michael nor did she adopt Michael. She was granted visitation by way of the divorce decree.

Conclusion:
I believe you have been duped by Ms. Vickers. I ask that you correct your records by closing out the missing person report and rescinding the warrant for my arrest. I request that you contact Missing Kids, inform them of this lie and ask that they cancel their poster action on me and my son. I request that you consider action against Ms. Vickers for filing a false police report. At the very least she needs to be called into your offices and clearly told that this sort of behavior will not be tolerated.

I further request that you respond to me on the resolution of this matter. You may contact me through the above listed address and telephone number. Thank you for your assistance and time.

Sincerely,

Robert D. Carey

ORIGINAL

PLANO POLICE
CUSTODY REPORT

~~CONFIDENTIAL
FOR
LAW ENFORCEMENT
USE ONLY~~

FILE # 0109 9717

ARRESTING OFC ID 155 5

DATE IN 10 - 09 - 01   TIME IN 1050 hrs.
LAST NAME Carey   FIRST Robert   MIDDLE Dean
ALIAS(ES) _____   MAIDEN _____
RACE white   SEX male   DOB 02084 HGT 6'7"   WGT 200   HAIR BRo   EYES GN
SSN 537 465345   DL NO 677257   DL ST OR   SCMD/TATTOOS Left thigh
BIRTHPLACE/ST WA.   OCCUPATION —
HOME ADDR 3304 Lacroc   EMPLOYER —   PHONE —
CITY Plano   ST 5   ZIP _____   ADDR —
PHONE 469-767-8070   CITY —   ST — ZIP —

CHARGES OR HOLDS	WARRANT NUMBER	BOND/FINE	AGENCY
1. Kidnapping	Cm 0120624	15000	Benton Co. So.
2. Flight to avoid pros.	—	- NO BOND	Portland FBI
3.	—	-	
4. —	—	-	
5. —	—	-	

WHERE ARRESTED 3300 Lacroc   DATE 10 089 01   TIME 1044 hrs.
WHERE COMMITTED —   DATE _____   TIME — hrs.
ASSOCIATES ARRESTED —
ASSOCIATES NOT ARRESTED —
VICTIM NAME —   ADDRESS —   CITY —
_____   HOME PHONE —   WORK PHONE —
VEH YR — MAKE — MOD — STYLE — COLOR — LIC YR — NO — ST —
VEHICLE IMPOUNDED Y/N IMPOUND TICKET # _____   STORED AT —

ARRAIGNMENT PROCEEDINGS

APPEARED BEFORE JUDGE _____
ON _____ AT _____ AM/PM

PLEAD:
   NOT GUILTY _____
   GUILTY _____
   NOLO CONTENDERE _____

FINES _____ BONDS _____
SERVED TIME _____ DAYS AT $ _____

ARREST # 1,657
JACKET # 1089 Si, CA
BEAT 232
RD 1272
APPROVED JHB
FAMILY VIOLENCE   YES _____   NO X   LKW
RELEASE INFO. RECEIPT# _____
HOW/TO. JB
DATE 10/9/01   TIME 0955
JAILER _____

ARRESTING OFFICER(S) Walker   ID # 1555

B-16

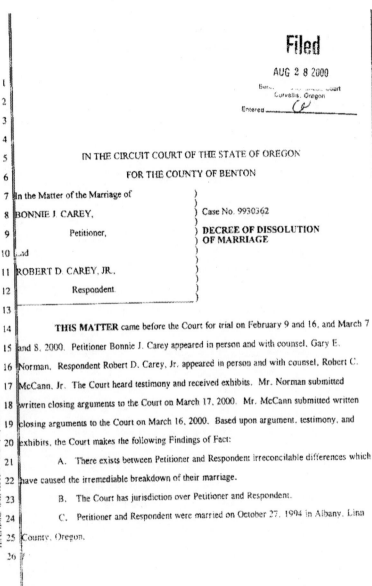

1   D. Wife is not now pregnant.

2   E. There are no children born as issue of this marriage.

3   F. Those facts required by ORS 107.085(3) are set forth in Exhibit 1 which is

4 attached hereto and by this reference incorporated herein and made a part of this Decree as

5 though fully set forth herein.

6   G. For a period of six (6) months immediately prior to the filing of her Petition for

7 Dissolution, Petitioner continuously has been and now is a resident and inhabitant of the state

8 of Oregon.

9   H. No domestic relations suits or petitions for support pursuant to ORS 107.110

10 involving this marriage of Petitioner and Respondent are pending in this or any other Court in

11 the state of Oregon or in any other state.

12   I. The Courts in the state of Oregon have exclusive jurisdiction to make child

13 custody determinations in this matter.

14   J. It is in the best interests of the minor child, Michael Robert Carey, born March

15 15, 1992, that his physical and legal custody be awarded to his father, the Respondent, Robert

16 D. Carey, Jr., subject to the parenting time of the Petitioner.

17   K. The Court in making its decision has prepared an Opinion Letter which has

18 additional Findings of Fact which are significant to the Court's decision in this matter. A copy

19 of that Opinion Letter is attached hereto, marked Exhibit 2, and by this reference incorporated

20 herein.

21   L. This marriage should be dissolved and Petitioner and Respondent should be

22 granted the relief hereinafter set forth.

23   **IT IS HEREBY ORDERED, ADJUDGED AND DECREED THAT:**

24   1. **Effective Date of Dissolution.** The marriage of the parties is dissolved

25 effective on the day of the signing of this Order by this Court.

26

3, BELAPIER, HEALY, McCANN, & NOONAN, P.C.
Attorneys at Law
201 West First Avenue, Suite 201 • P.O. Box 40
Albany, OR 97321-0014
TELEPHONE: (541) 926-5504 • FAX: (541) 926-7167

Page 2 - DECREE OF DISSOLUTION OF MARRIAGE
Carey and Carey

2. **Child Custody and Parenting Plan.** Respondent Robert D. Carey, Jr. is awarded custody of the minor child, Michael Robert Carey, born March 15, 1992.

2.1. Petitioner is a psychological parent of Michael Robert Carey and is entitled to parenting time with Michael Robert Carey. That parenting time should be pursuant to the standard Benton County Parenting Plan, a copy of which is attached hereto, marked Exhibit 3, and by this reference incorporated herein.

2.1.1. The standard Benton County Parenting Plan shall be modified as follows in this situation:

2.1.1.1. During the school's summer vacation period, the parties shall alternate parenting time on a weekly basis instead of two-week block as set forth in the Benton County schedule. All exchanges of Michael's physical custody during the summer vacation period will be in accordance with the Benton County schedule (exchanges at 4:00 p.m.).

2.1.1.2. During the school year and as long as the Respondent and child live in Albany and the Petitioner works near the child's daycare facility, the Petitioner shall initiate visitation with Michael Robert Carey at 4:00 p.m. When the Respondent and child move and this is no longer possible, visitation will revert to the standard Benton County schedule.

2.2. Until further order of the Court, Respondent's residence must be within sixty (60) miles of Petitioner's current residence to facilitate Petitioner's parenting time with Michael.

G, DELAFOER, HEALY, McCANN, & NOONAN, P.C.
Attorneys at Law
201 West First Avenue, Suite 201 • P.O. Box 40
Albany, OR 97321-0014
TELEPHONE: (541) 926-5804 • FAX: (541) 926-3167

Page 3 - DECREE OF DISSOLUTION OF MARRIAGE
Carey and Carey

IN THE CIRCUIT COURT FOR THE STATE OF OREGON COUNTY OF BENTON

STATE OF OREGON,

Plaintiff,

v.

Robert Dean Carey

Defendant.

Judge: Robert S. Gardner

Reporter: N. Jenson

Date: 1/28/02

SENTENCE JUDGMENT

Case # CM01-20629

Count # Custodial Interference I - Count 1

Crime Contempt of Court - Count 2

State's Atty: Dan Armstrong

Defendant's Atty: Stephen R. Ensor

Incident Date: April 9, 2001

DEFENDANT: by phone

(X) Appeared in person (X) with counsel ( ) waived representation by an attorney after having been informed of that right.

(X) Was arraigned and advised of his/her rights and the maximum possible penalties.

(X) Entered plea(s) of ( ) guilty (X) no contest to the above charge(s) and waived further time for imposition of sentence. — Contempt of Court - Count 2

( ) Appeared for sentencing upon the previously entered ( ) verdict(s) of guilty ( ) plea(s) of guilty ( ) plea(s) of no contest to the above charge(s).

COURT FINDINGS: Defendant's plea was made freely and voluntarily and there is a factual and legal basis for the plea and the plea shall be entered of record herein.

IT IS ORDERED AND ADJUDGED: Oral record is incorporated into this Judgment.

(X) Upon oral motion of the State, Count(s) _1_ of the accusatory instrument is/are dismissed.

(X) Upon conviction for _Contempt of Court_, Count _2_, (X) Imposition of sentence is suspended and Defendant placed on probation for _18 months_ years under the supervision of (X) this Court
( ) Benton County Community Corrections. Report to Probation Office by 4:00 PM today.
( ) Not on probation - straight sentence.
( ) Upon successful completion of all conditions of probation, Defendant may request early termination after ____ months.

( ) Upon conviction for _____, Count _____, ( ) Imposition of sentence is suspended and Defendant placed on probation for ____ months/years under the supervision of ( ) this Court
( ) Benton County Community Corrections. Report to Probation Office by 4:00 PM today.
( ) Not on probation - straight sentence.
( ) Upon successful completion of all conditions of probation, Defendant may request early termination after ____ months.

DEFENDANT SHALL BE SUBJECT TO THE FOLLOWING CONDITIONS OF PROBATION:

Defendant shall obey all laws, Federal, State, and Municipal and must at all times keep this Court advised in writing of his/her current address, telephone number, and current employer.

(X) GENERAL CONDITIONS OF SUPERVISED PROBATION: as set forth in attachment to this judgment.

(X) JAIL: Defendant shall serve _45_ days/months in the Benton County Corrections Facility (BCCF) and shall report to arrange time to be served by 4:00 PM today. _45_ days suspended on condition _pay full restitution_ _to Bonnie Vickers as determined by court at separate restitution hearing._
( ) Credit time served. ( ) Sentence shall be concurrent/consecutive to sentence in _____

( ) WORK CREW: ( ) In lieu of ____ days in BCCF, Defendant shall/may perform ____ days on the Benton County Work Crew as directed by the Coordinator to whom Defendant shall report by 4:00 PM today. Work Crew to be completed ( ) at the rate of at least 2 days work crew every 30 days ( ) within _____

( ) HOME DETENTION: ( ) In lieu of ____ days in BCCF, Defendant shall/may serve ____ days Home Detention if approved by the Coordinator to whom Defendant shall report by 4:00 PM today. Home Detention to begin on or before _____

( ) COMMUNITY SERVICE: Defendant shall perform ____ hours community service to be completed ( ) at the rate of at least 12 hours per month ( ) within _____. Defendant shall report to the Coordinator by 4:00 PM today. Defendant shall provide proof from the agency to this Court.

( ) **EVALUATION/TREATMENT:** Defendant shall, at his/her expense, complete an evaluation and treatment program for _____ as directed by ( ) Probation Officer ( ) George Baskerville, (541) 752-3820.
( ) Benton County Mental Health, ( ) Community Outreach, including residential treatment if directed.

( ) **ASSOCIATIONS:** Defendant shall not associate with ( ) any persons known to be engaged in criminal activities
( ) persons under the age of _____ ( ) Co-Defendants _____
( ) Victim and/or family of the victim _____
( ) Other _____
( ) **FREQUENTING:** Defendant shall not knowingly be with persons or in places where controlled substances are unlawfully kept, used, or sold.

( ) Defendant shall not operate a motor vehicle without valid license or permit and insurance.

( ) Defendant's Oregon Driver's License and right to apply therefor is suspended for _____

Defendant may be considered for any form of temporary leave from custody, reduction of sentence, work release, alternative incarceration program or program conditional release authorized by law for which the Defendant is otherwise eligible.

( ) Write letter of apology to _____ and submit to the Court within _____

(✗) **OTHER:** *No contact with son Michael Corey, unless approved by Court in pending dissolution case.*

Defendant shall seek and maintain gainful employment and pay the financial obligations imposed below.

MONEY JUDGMENT

Judgment Creditor: State of Oregon
Judgment Debtor: Defendant (named in case caption)
    Ct __ Ct __

		Payee: *Restitution Hrg 2/12 @ 2:15 p.m.*
Unitary Assessment:	$ *65*	*Restitution to be determined at hearing.*
Restitution:	$	
DUII Assessment:	$	
Court Costs:	$	(Restitution to be paid to the Court and disbursed by the Court Clerk)
Attorney Fees:	$	( ) Joint and Several with: _____ Case # _____
Fine:	$	
County Assessment:	$	
TOTAL:	$ *65 + restitution* Less security/bail posted in this case, if any.

If a period of time is given in which to pay financial obligations, a payment schedule assessment will be imposed in the amount of $25 for obligations totaling $1-$100 and in the amount of $50 for obligations totaling more than $100.

$_____ of the fine is suspended ( ) on condition that Defendant comply with all conditions of this probation ( ) enter into and successfully complete evaluation and treatment as directed ( ) complete _____ hours of community service at minimum wage by _____ ( ) if Defendant produces a valid Oregon Driver's License and proof of insurance by _____

Suspended Fines - payments must continue to be made until Defendant provides the Court with proof that conditions of probation have been completed **before** fines will be suspended.

( ) Defendant must report to the Court Accounting Office, Room 111, by 4:00 PM on _____

PAYMENTS: Shall be made payable to State of Oregon and mailed to Benton County Circuit Court, P. O. Box 1870, Corvallis, OR, 97339.

    $_____ per month beginning _____ To be paid with Case # _____
    $_____ in full by _____
    ( ) Payment plan to be set by Probation Officer.

Dated this *28* day of *January*, 200*2*

_____
Circuit Court Judge   ( ) pro tem
Robert S. Gardner

this technique was discussed with her today. Lastly, in light of Michael's recent abduction, it is recommended that he continue with counseling, which has already been initiated.

DIAGNOSES:
  1.   Autism.
  2.   Mental retardation.
  3.   Mild gross motor delay.
  4.   Speech delay.

PLAN:
  1.   Greenspan's Floor Time and Speech Development Program – information about this program was introduced to Michael's stepmother today, and she received information about further training in this program.
  2.   Occupational Therapy and Physical Therapy evaluations – these should be performed at Michael's school, to further investigate and evaluate his mild fine motor and gross motor delays.
  3.   One-on-one tutoring and help at school – this should be continued, as it has been initiated already.
  4.   Identify and inform Michael's stepmother about various community services and support groups for autism, including the Council on Autism.
  5.   Continue counseling.

Sean McCormick, M.D.
Resident, Pediatrics

Phillip M. Brenes, M.D.
Associate Professor,
Pediatrics
SM:x50
D: 03/04/2002
T: 03/04/2002
001442088

Oregon Health & Science University Consultative Report CHILD DEVELOPMENT AND REHABILITATION CENTER P.O. Box 574, Portland OR 97207-0574	Account No Medical Record No. 01-47-67-11 Name Carey, Michael R Birthdate 03/15/1992

CLINIC DATE: 03/04/2002

CLINIC NAME: CHILD DEVELOPMENT CLINIC

DISCIPLINE: PSYCHOLOGY

IDENTIFYING INFORMATION: Michael Carey is a nine-year, 11-month-old white boy who lives with his stepmother in Albany. He is enrolled in the fourth grade at North Albany Elementary School. He receives special education services in academics and speech and language with Educational Autism as a qualifying condition.

PRESENTING PROBLEMS: Michael's stepmother and custodial parent, Bonnie Jay Vickers, is seeking confirmation of the findings of the EIP, including the level of his cognitive abilities. He has been diagnosed with autism which is manifested in academic and language delays. Ms. Vickers wishes to proceed for planning with Michael and needs a medical diagnosis to seek Mental Health Division (MHD) eligibility for services in the future. In addition, a motion is before the Benton County Court in regard to a modification of the parenting plan and Ms. Vickers was aware of the importance of documenting Michael's special needs.

PERTINENT HISTORY: Ms. Vickers reports that Michael's birth mother died of cancer when he was two years old and she came into his life about that time, in 1994. She and Michael's father divorced in August of 2000. Ms. Vickers had assumed primary responsibility for Michael's care following the divorce and under Oregon Statute was found to be the psychological parent. Michael's father engaged in custodial interference in April 2000, and Michael was returned to Ms. Vickers' care from Texas, where the child had been located by the FBI. In interview today, Ms. Vickers reported that Michael has been greatly distressed by his removal from his mother's home. He can relate to her anecdotes about being on the move with his father and since his return in late summer, has been adamant that he and Ms. Vickers not leave home. Ms. Vickers and Michael have been engaged in family counseling to address the disruption in their lives, occasioned by his abduction. They met approximately five times on a weekly basis with a private counselor and now have sessions once a month.

Psychoeducational assessments were not available to the present writer at the time of the examination. Michael attended a private kindergarten and apparently had an IEP for the primary grades, which included a full-time Special Education assistant. The reader is referred to the Special Education consultation completed by LizBeth Saylor, M.S. as part of today's clinic visit.

BEHAVIORAL OBSERVATIONS: Michael appeared as a handsome older child, appearing to be tall for his age, with blond hair and blue eyes. He was quick to establish eye contact with the examiner upon first meeting, but his rote greeting was confounded by his introduction of seeming gibberish. His mother explains that Michael has a language of his own which is not intelligible as English words.

He easily separated from his mother and went with the examiner to the consulting office. Later in the session, he became anxious about her and needed to check on her, and then was reassured. The quality of his performance on the standardized intelligence Test was highly uneven. He had particular difficulty with word finding on the *Picture Completion* subtest, in which he has to name a part that is missing.

3.2 / CD-1150E

CLINIC DATE: 03/04/2002   Med Rec No.: 01-67-67-11
Page 3   Name: Carey, Michael R

surroundings and it is not clear if this the disruption in his socialization related to his autism or the result of traumatization due to the custodial interference.

FORMULATION: Michael Carey appears to be a child with highly evident characteristics of autism. His recent adjustment has been recently compromised by his being taken from his psychological parent's care by his father, and having been separated from his mother for an extended period approximately six months ago. He is reported to be anxious as a result of this; however, in the course of today's clinic visit he appeared to make sustained efforts to work with a series of adults who were previously unknown to him. Michael can be engaged and evidences a pleasant, if limited, interactional style.

RECOMMENDATIONS:
1.   **Educational Placement.** Educators are encouraged to continue in the current IEP and it is recommended that physical therapy and occupational therapy evaluations be undertaken in the relatively near future.
2.   **Mental Health Services.** Ms. Vickers should apply to the MHD through the County Mental Health Program so that Michael might be eligible for services in case management, respite care, and long-term planning.
3.   **Parent Services.** Ms. Vickers has already availed herself of opportunities for family counseling. She may appreciate additional opportunities for education and parent training through the Counsel on Autism or other parent advocate groups serving individuals with autism and their family.

It was a delight to work with Michael and Ms. Vickers in the course of today's clinic visit. Questions or comments may be directed to me at (503) 870-9309. Time dedicated in the completion of the examination reported above is three hours.

Susan W Horton

Susan W. Horton, Ph.D.
Clinical Psychologist

SWH:x76
D: 03/04/2002
T: 03/05/2002
C: 03/08/2002 swh
001442275

APPENDIX C

Other Books That Might Help

The following is a list of other books on the topic of divorce and child custody issues. They include:

A Family Divided: A Divorced Father's Struggle with the Child Custody Industry by Robert Mendelson (**Prometheus Books**, 1997)

In *A Family Divided* author Robert Mendelson, a freelance writer, presents the divorced father's point of view, arguing that fathers are not superfluous and not all of them should be considered "deadbeat dads" who shirk their parental responsibilities. Moreover, public opinion, the press, and the courts are wrong to believe that men cannot be single parents; that a parental role can be fulfilled through sporadic weekend visits.

Divorced Dads: Shattering the Myths by Sanford L. Braver (**Penguin USA**, 1998)

In this revolutionary work, psychologist Sanford L. Braver shows how millions of well-intentioned parents, judges, lawyers, educators, and other caregivers have been repeatedly and tragically misled by the most widely accepted social data about divorce and parenthood. For years, our society has accepted the image of "deadbeat dads" who shirk child-support payments and other responsibilities. *Divorced Dads* posits a new, more hopeful idea of how parenting can function after a split, with the more active participation of a father figure.

Still a Dad: The Divorced Father's Journey by Serge Prengel (**Mission Creative Energy Inc.**, 1999)

Still A Dad provides a much-needed look at the experience of divorce from the father's point of view. This book gives us a "look" inside the heart and mind of a typical divorced father, John Doe, during and after his break-up with wife Jane. John's story is that of a developmental process the readers can emulate. John starts out confused, hurt and angry; then finds a focus that allows him to rebuild himself and be a good father to his child.

Fighting for Your Children*: A Father's Guide to Custody* by John Steinbreder (**Taylor Publishing Company**, 1998)

In recent years, more fathers have attempted to win custody of their children following a divorce. In "Fighting for Your Children," the authors help men who are facing such a battle, guiding them through the entire legal experience. Using anecdotes from fathers who have successfully gained full or joint custody of their children as well as from fathers who have met with failure, this book illustrates the do's and don'ts of waging a custody battle for children.

Winning Your Divorce*: A Man's Survival Guide* by Timothy J. Horgan (**Penguin USA**, 1995)

This essential book of strategy for dealing with the legal aspects of divorce is the only up-to-date book of its kind for men. Written by a successful divorce lawyer, it guides husbands step-by-step through all the pitfalls possible during this difficult time. Dedicated to helping the reader emerge from divorce with sanity and economic assets relatively intact, the book views the process of divorce as a competitive struggle in which there are two participants and where eventual victory goes to the party who is better prepared.

Father's Rights*: Hard-hitting and Fair Advice for Every Father Involved in a Custody Dispute* by Jeffery M. Leving (**Perseus Books**, 1998)

Millions of fathers are currently in the fight of their lives: the fight for custody of their children. Many wonder if they will ever again be an important part of their children's lives. With this landmark book, renowned men's rights attorney Jeffery Leving leads fathers through every twist and turn of the legal system, offering meaningful advice to save years of anguish and possibly thousands of dollars.

About the Authors

Robert Carey is a man on a mission. Having survived an intense legal battle and earned debilitating scars from the experience, he is eager to share his story with other fathers—and mothers—out there who may be suffering the same cruel twist of fate at the hands of those they once loved so dearly.

Widowed after the death of his beloved wife when his son was only two-years-old, remarried, divorced and then betrayed by his vengeful ex-wife, raising a highly-functioning autistic son on his own, vilified by his ex-wife in their small community, arrested on trumped up charges, severely burdened by staggering legal fees, and rendered powerless by the nearsighted Oregon court system, Robert continues to fight—for his *own* child—against incredible odds.

When his soon-to-be ex-wife first told Robert she wanted a divorce, he was shocked. A Christian man to whom the words "'til death do us part" are more than a vow, but a way of life, Robert did all he could to make the marriage work—to no avail. As his soon-to-be ex-wife's behavior toward his biological son soon became more than he could bear, a divorce eventually seemed inevitable. Finally, that inevitability became a reality.

But the divorce he had dreaded soon became the tip of a legal iceberg that would find him searching his soul for the very meaning of justice. Robert's ex-wife would soon take advantage of an Oregon legal term, *psychological parent*: "The person whom the child understands to be their parent, and to whom the child is accustomed to relying upon for care-taking, need not be biological parent."

After the divorce, Robert took his ex-wife to court for relief from her constant harassment and, eventually, contempt of court. The court virtually ignored both issues, leaving a dismayed Robert with few options. At the time, Robert felt that his only recourse was to leave the state, even though that would put him in contempt of court.

The divorce decree clearly gave Robert physical and legal custody of his son, but the District Attorney, unfamiliar with divorce law, believed his ex-wife's falsified claim of joint custody and ignored that fact of law. With the DA's help, Robert's ex-wife filed a false police report and lied to the courts to improve her situation. She maliciously brought a false felony charge against Robert so that he would be put in jail—and his son would be placed into *her* custody. Robert soon found himself giving over his biological son to a woman whom he couldn't trust.

A free man today, Robert has since remarried and enjoys the peaceful life he now leads with his new wife and stepchildren. As one would imagine, there is still an empty space in his heart for young Michael. He has vowed to win custody of his child, and is now, for the first time, telling his story in that attempt.

And what a story it is!

Multi-published co-author Rusty Fischer has written over thirty books for such reputable publishers as **McGraw-Hill, Lebhar-Friedman Books, Weyant Press, Mason Crest Publishers**, and **Frank Schaffer Publications**. Over 100 of his essays, stories, tips, and ideas have appeared in such nationally recognized periodicals as *Good Housekeeping, Better Homes & Gardens*, and *Seventeen* magazine. His stories have been anthologized in such bestsellers as *Chicken Soup for the Soul* (**HCI**), *A Cup of Comfort* (**Adams Media**), *A Gift of Miracles* (**HarperCollins**), *The Heart of a Father* (**Bethany House**), and *God Allows U-turns* (**Barbour Publishing**).

0-595-27390-4